SURVIVING IN A RUTHLESS WORLD

RUTHLESS WORLD

Bob Dylan's Voyage to Infidels

Terry Gans

FIRST PUBLISHED BY RED PLANET BOOKS IN 2020

TEXT COPYRIGHT © TERRY GANS 2020

THIS EDITION COPYRIGHT © RED PLANET BOOKS 2020

Printed in the UK by TJ Books

ISBN: 978 1 9127 3339 2

redplanetbooks

Red Planet Books, PO Box 355, Falmouth TR11 9ER   redplanetbooks.co.uk

Cover design / Winlong Hong Cover photo / Lynn Goldsmith/Corbis/VCG via Getty Images

For the future ...

... Jason, Aaron, Evan, Eliza
and Willa.

FOREWORD

By the fall of 1983, there had been nearly a year of speculation regarding Bob Dylan considering, preparing and recording an album of new songs. It had been two years since the artist had released new material and I was hungry for it. In the days before the internet, scraps of information came by way of *Rolling Stone's* 'Random Notes', or letters from friends with similar interests. The news, rumors actually, was piecemeal and often unreliable.

Suddenly, the waiting and imagining was at an end. An album was completed and would be titled *Infidels*. I first heard it from a bootlegged cassette sent by a long-forgotten contact. The first note from the forthcoming album set what now seems to me an inevitable course from early October 1983 to this book. The album's music had a seductively different sound and was a world apart from the strident sound of its predecessor, 1981's *Shot of Love*. The lyrics were infused with that hallmark Dylan vagueness. The singing voice was another in a long history of guises and was almost embracing in its pull.

Infidels was released on October 27. Not many days later, a longer bootleg tape began to circulate. It included songs obviously recorded at the same sessions as the album, but not included on it. There was nearly another album's worth of great songs. And to add to the intrigue of the forbidden fruit, some of the versions of the released songs had different lyrics. All of this was a puzzle, the impact of which took root and grew over the next thirty-four years. The different lyrics and additional songs remained a thing of mystery until, seemingly out of the blue, a resource became available in 2016 which provided an avenue for research and sorting much of it out.

Almost no one imagined Dylan had an archive. Or that such a collection would have been offered for acquisition. But this was the case, and the George Kaiser Family Foundation, in concert with the University of Tulsa, purchased the materials and established The Bob Dylan Archive®.

In 1983, though, all of this was far in the unforeseeable future.

When any writer tackles an article or a book about Bob Dylan, he or she soon comes to a fork in the mental road: Am I going to try to get inside Dylan's head? Am I going to venture into, as he said in 'Gates of Eden', "the ditch of what each one means?" For the purposes of this book, those paths would be a fool's journey. In Joan Baez' interview for the Martin Scorsese–directed documentary *No Direction Home*, Baez remembered a young and still-evolving Dylan saying, "See now, a bunch of years from now, all these people, all these assholes are gonna be writing about all the shit I write. I don't know where the fuck it comes from. I don't know what the fuck it's about. And they're gonna write what it's about."[1]

Dylan's writing is prismatic, with possible meanings refracted by the light each brings at the time of hearing or reading. People interviewed in this book, to a person, say such things as "there's a zillion sides to Bob Dylan."

I will do my best to avoid hopeless traps like 'Bob must have thought' or 'Here is what Dylan meant.' In following the evolution of the album *Infidels*, my hope is to stick to facts: the drafts, notebook jottings. There is plenty to sift through – it's prospecting as in 'Days of '49', with tin pan and floppy hat included. This prospecting claim comes with the addition of the material at the Bob Dylan Archive in Tulsa. Where there is evidence that an experience or exposure may have influenced Dylan's work, I will present it as something to be considered. All speculation, or connecting the dots, is meant to provoke the reader and is not presented as gospel.

The research for this project has yielded a rich trove of clues as the songs for Infidels progressed from the germ of composition, to recording, to release or abandonment. We can all study clues, we can all enjoy songs and we can all cherish the journey of interpretation. To paraphrase; if you want a meaning you can trust, trust yourself. But that doesn't mean you'll be spared my opinions. After all, we're all "these people, these assholes."

Mark Knopfler intended the sessions to be fun. I want this book to be fun. Please have it.

Terry Gans
Longboat Key, FL
June 2020

---

1 / Martin Scorsese, dir. *No Direction Home*. HBO, 2005

PROLOGUE

When Infidels arrived in late 1983, it followed a two-year near-total absence of Bob Dylan from performing or studio recording. There was a one-off three-song duet with Joan Baez at a massive anti-nuke rally in Pasadena in June 1982, including Jimmy Buffet's 'A Pirate Looks at Forty'.[2] Dylan was also photographed the month before attending a funeral for Buddha Records founder Neil Bogart. But apart from that, and allegedly hitting a photographer at the Los Angeles airport, and attending concerts in Los Angeles and Minneapolis, Dylan kept out of the public eye.

For a good deal of that time, Dylan was out to sea – literally. He, along with a partner, had begun sailing on his boat, which they began constructing in 1977. And it was no run-of-the mill vessel. Handcrafted from specially selected woods imported to the Caribbean island of Bequia, the 68-foot sail-and-engine-powered Water Pearl was constructed on the beach and launched in December 1980. She likely visited most of the ports in the Antilles, Grenadines, Jamaica and Barbados. How many of these stops Dylan was on board for is unclear. But there is good evidence that in the latter part of 1982 and January 1983, while writing and preparing for the April recording of a new album, he was sailing around St. Vincent, St. Barts, St. Martin and Anguilla.

Sea air, blue skies, and turquoise waters created, if not peace of mind, a spirit that would infuse his writings of that time in terms of language and music. On land, the conversations Dylan engaged in and overheard floated into the notes he was making and the lines he was sketching, while nurturing the gift that would coalesce thoughts into the framework of songs.

Who traveled with Dylan? Where specifically did he go and when? Certainly, for purposes of a complete historical record, it would be good to know. But we don't have to. We can imagine his drifting on the seas, where there were no executives or studio clocks or reporters demanding his attention. Warm days and nights. Gentle waters. Fishing and lobstering. Just relaxing, Dylan was writing in one of the small notebooks he always seemed to have on hand,

2 / Dylan had the lyrics written on his arm or sleeve

mixing life with imagination. He allowed the sounds of the Islands to seep into the rhythm of his writing and the music he envisioned for the writings. There was no internet, no Facebook, no TMZ to spy and distract. There was simply the sea, the shore, pencil, paper, guitar, eyes and ears..words, lots of words, lots of play with the words, trying to get it to feel right. He could think about musicians who could provide texture to the songs and a producer who could harness the intricacies of the studio and bring the project to a good conclusion.

On a preliminary basis, it probably seemed like the right process. But the project would require lots of effort, change, work and even more change. The endpoint would never be the starting point. Polish the songs, then refine some more in the studio. Wrap it up. Then go back and redo a lot of it. Put a name on the collection and design the cover. And delay the release to change both.

And when all is ready to be presented to the world, what does the world receive? Great sounding music played by great musicians. Words that provoked different responses with each listening. Beneath the surface of the seductive sound though was a spirit of dread and a mirror reflected back on everyone. A scowling face framed by a car window formed an album cover. Inside was a picture of Bob Dylan kneeling on a Jerusalem hill. Was his expression reverence or despair?[3]

Most initial reviews were positive. Some were ecstatic. The album sold well in its initial release, better than its predecessor. It reached number 20 on the Billboard charts. But over time, Infidels has not found a comfortable spot in Dylan's recorded legacy. It seems to have been stranded among the three born-again albums that preceded it, the debate about the excellent songs left off the album and the declining inspiration for and performance on the three albums that followed. The consideration of the album as a standalone artistic entity was also clouded by the ever-present questioning of where Dylan's religious convictions lay.

This book seeks to make Infidels' place in Dylan's resume clearer.

Infidels sounds like no other album in Bob Dylan's career, either musically or lyrically. It is neither a renunciation of what came before or a direct link

---

3 / Both photos were reported to have been taken in Israel in Summer 1983

to what followed. It is consistent however with Dylan's attitude toward the world and the nature of humanity.

If we only had the eight songs on the album, that would have been sufficient. But eight additional songs were recorded but left off the album. And, as of 2016, thirty-three years later, we have the in Tulsa, Oklahoma. The Archives provided the resources to study the possible genesis of the ideas that wound up as songs.

Documents show the development of lyrics through numerous drafts over many months. It is possible to eavesdrop on the month of recording sessions, as songs emerged and evolved and mutated over some 400 stops and starts and complete takes.

The released Infidels album is the tip of the iceberg. Underneath is the enormous effort of a determined artist. The question as to whether the album's unity of spirit was Dylan's original purpose or was the result of his subconscious is not in a file in the archive. The researcher can only follow the evidence of the development and the final choices made. After that it's a matter of interpretation.

HOW THIS BOOK IS STRUCTURED

This book is intended as an objective history of a work of art. As true art is the result of inspiration and labor, a straight line and logical order is difficult or impossible to achieve The research for the book includes plenty of facts, lots of first-hand recollections from those who were there, and a helping of contemporaneous rumor. All are rich source material. At times in the research, a large portion of what happened was established, but the why it happened or what the motivation was led by informed speculation. Where such suppositions, are presented, I provide an alternate hypothesis. In all cases, speculation is identified as such. The reader can choose which speculation seems more likely or reject it entirely.

Interviews, both primary and previously published, given by the participants and Dylan himself, are an important resource. But any interview and many conversations are a performance. In an interview, the subject is trying to provide a particular version of him/herself. What is said may be presented to please the interviewer or to project an image or point of view to the audience. Responses may range from truth, as the subject sees it, or game-playing. Lines that worked before may be used again. New ideas expressed at one specific moment might never be said again or even considered. Each interview is just a part of the overall mosaic, not truth etched in stone.

Chapters explore how Dylan spent his time prior to and while writing the songs for *Infidels*, how the musical and production team came into place, the technical choices they made and the recording and production process Interviewees memories breathe life into the narrative and deliver a feel of the process and how the participants interacted.

After the foundation is firmly in place, the 18 complete *Infidels* songs are presented, one-by-one. Each song is discussed in terms of written lyrics, the recording of the song, often over different days and sessions, and the choices that were made regarding the final version. A lot of other music recorded in the nearly 30 hours of digital session tape, and additional hours of continually running analogue tapes, is covered after the 18 song presentations. Appendices follow conclusions and lay out the session and post-session chronology. this is followed by a list of clichés in the lyrics, a bibliography and acknowledgements.

Section One:

The Beginings

1:

The Boat and the Notebooks

What do we know about Bob Dylan? What do we really know? Dylan has had a near 60-year career. Hundreds of books have been published on his life, his music, his art and his interviews. And those are just the ones in English. These are not relics of the Sixties. New books marketed as major works are released each year. Dozens of Dylan-centric magazines have come and gone, and several are in publication to this day. Page after page and tree after tree have been sacrificed trying to understand the man behind decades of public work in the recording studio, on film, in concerts (playing to at least 300,000 people each year), in jousts with journalists, and as the subject of countless photographs.

What do we know beyond the surface? What was Moses' favorite meal? What was Jesus' sandal size? What was the name of Lincoln's doctor's dog? Of the 525,600 minutes in a year, how many does anyone witness of another? How many of those minutes provide evidence of the person? How much, if any, of what we witness contributes to an accurate picture? Dylan's concerts themselves consume about 11,000 minutes a year. Photographs capture a split-second of that time.

The narrator of 'Idiot Wind' complains about "images and distorted facts". Provocative quotes, pulled from longer works, are repeated and headlined, become defining: "He not busy being born is busy dying; Something is happening; The Times They Are A-Changin'; That must be what it's all about." And on and on.

What do we know about Bob Dylan? We know his work. What is on his records, films, and books. We can find what he's said and what he's done in public. Beyond that, we guess. We surmise. We speculate. And we project.

Robert Zimmerman created Bob Dylan. He may or may not have created the Dylan myth, but he most certainly abetted and used it. To some extent he and we are, to various extents, prisoners on opposite sides of that myth.

Infidels

Infidels did appear out of nowhere. While stylistically it was a departure, every album in Dylan's career has been a departure. The three albums which immediately preceded Infidels were infused with songs reflecting concepts of Christian faith. Over time, they have been labeled as Dylan's Gospel Trilogy:

Slow Train Coming, Saved, and *Shot of Love*: The first two have uniformly overt religious content, specifically how Dylan related to the concept of Jesus Christ being Lord and Savior. Whether Dylan experienced a supernatural touch, underwent a formal conversion, or simply immersed himself into learning and exploring as much about salvation as he could is unknowable and probably irrelevant when considering the art that resulted.

In *Shot of Love* the songs focus on judgement and reflection about himself ('Shot of Love', 'Heart of Mine,' 'Every Grain of Sand', 'In The Summertime',), how others judged him ('Property of Jesus'), a misguided world ('Watered-Down Love', 'Trouble', 'The Groom's Still Waiting At the Altar', 'Dead Man Dead Man') and one which could be any of the three ('Lenny Bruce'). While the initial two albums could be considered as calls to the Lord, the third was commentary. While *Shot of Love* had its toe dipped into the secular world, Dylan wrote the songs with a lot of ink drawn from the New Testament.

Even this trilogy had precedents. Practically from the moment Robert Zimmerman became Bob Dylan, the attraction of speaking/singing with the voice of a prophet seemed an instinctive path. Thus, we have early songs such as 'I'd Hate to Be You on That Dreadful Day', 'Quit Your Lowdown Ways', 'Whatcha Gonna Do', 'A Hard Rain's A Gonna Fall', and When the Ship Comes In'. Individual verses in many songs are sprinkled with this voice.

Some fans and some critics viewed him as a prophet. This put a pressure on Dylan for which he was unprepared and which he quickly decided he did not want. His songwriting turned inward, beginning in late 1963, although the songs he performed in concerts for the next two years included a good number of his earlier rallying cries, particularly 'The Times They Are A' Changin', which is rich in biblical phrasing. By late-1965, his concerts almost totally consisted of symbolic and, to some listeners, incomprehensible song-poems he had written and recorded since June 1964.

Dylan's increasingly wild music reflected a chaotic lifestyle until a crash of some sort – motorcycle, psychological or both – put an end to that chapter.

The album which followed, *John Wesley Harding*, is a summing-up by a good man who strayed from his path. Indeed, Dylan indicated in the album's songs and liner notes that he was lured from his rightful path. He wanted out and did so through possibly miraculous intervention. He pleaded in his new songs to be left alone, to regain his footing and expressed a compassion and forgiveness toward others. By the album's final two songs, the prophet and sage had disappeared, replaced by a country crooner.

The three years that followed saw a continuation of the country-styled recordings begun with *John Wesley Harding*, including one collection that in Dylan's revisionist telling was intended to alienate his audience. It was a good story to explain the curious June 1970 album *Self Portrait*, but whatever the scheme, it was countered by another release, *New Morning*, within five months that more closely met fans and critics expectations.

One of the most respected critics, Ralph Gleason, who enjoyed the reputation as a preeminent writer on things rock and jazz, went over the top, with "We've got Dylan back again." What we got was an album that fit in with his personal projections of how Dylan should write and sing, although some of the la-la-la-ing did give pause for thought to some. That the album closed with the hymn-like 'Father of Night' that demonstrated that Dylan had not abandoned themes suggesting there was someone or something out there.

Within a year or so, he had composed 'Forever Young', which mirrored a biblical prayer of benediction. This song was included – twice – on the album *Planet Waves*, released to coincide with his first tour in eight years. It was a good collection of songs and seemed aimed at receiving the Lord's benediction for his children, but even more so to convince his wife of his love for her.

How well that worked can be heard in the brutally beautiful *Blood on the Tracks*. According to most who heard it, it chronicled the pain of marital rupture. In Dylan's own book of autobiographical recollections, *Chronicles Part One*, he says *Blood on the Tracks* was based on a collection of Chekov stories. While some still labor to figure out which Chekov stories these might be. *Blood on the Tracks* may arguably be one of the finest works of recorded art ever produced. On second thoughts, strike the 'maybe'.

The album *Desire* which followed continued the marital tale to some degree, and ended with the plea, "Don't ever leave me, don't ever go".

Dylan was newly divorced in 1977, and before recording the lyrically dense and spiritually unfocussed *Street Legal*, put together a four-hour movie – *Renaldo and Clara*. The film tackled the Dylan myth (created, of course, by

Dylan), the question of identity, and is laden with religious images, especially Christian symbols. In the movie, a street preacher harangues a crowd in downtown New York, scenes depicted numerous crucifixes, a fragment of a song 'What Will You Do When Jesus Comes' is heard, and it concluded with a performance of 'Knockin' on Heaven's Door.' Indeed, looking back, it does seem that a door was opened to something.

What entered that door was at the very least a fascination with the concept of Jesus and salvation. Dylan has claimed he never used the term 'born again', and perhaps never truly embraced the concept. Whatever, the experience and/or fascination, it led to the aforementioned trilogy, and, from November 1979 to April 1980, some of the greatest concert performances Dylan ever gave. The religious nature of the songs and strength of delivery cannot be denied, and anyone who has not witnessed his performance in those concerts should get a copy of *Trouble No More*, the recordings and film covering this period.

By September 1980 at the latest, Dylan embarked on eight months of writing and recording songs more centered on secular and personal concerns, spiritual for sure but not directly laden with evangelical messages. For one thing, Dylan had been told in no uncertain terms, "No More" by Columbia Records.[4] Whether such corporate dictates would cause Dylan to do something he did not already want to do is dubious. But whatever proselytizing that continued was left for listeners to read between the lines.

Musically, by the time of the *Shot of Love* album, the accompaniment had gone from gently embracing revival gospel to in your face rock. Dylan's vocals were far to the front and delivered higher in his vocal register, often punctuated by "huh-uh" at the end of lines. Summer- fall 1981 tour concerts ran, at tours' end, to thirty songs. Only seven of those were from *Slow Train Coming* or *Saved*. Dylan was moving on.

---

4 / An oft-repeated and completely unverified tale by former Yardbirds and Wham manager Simon Napier-Bell of an overheard phone call by CBS Records co-head Dick Asher to Dylan "No fucking religion—not Christian, not Jewish, not Muslim. Nothing" Clinton Heylin Trouble in Mind (New York: Lesser Gods, 2017),173 Arma Andon, a Columbia executive during the Seventies and Eighties considers such a harangue from Asher possible, and that rumors were that label President Walter Yetnikoff was not pleased over the incident

Sailing

Dylan was in Tucson, Arizona touring behind the first of his gospel trilogy albums when an event thousands of miles away occurred that would influence Infidels four years later. On December 9, 1979, Patty Perkins broke the traditional bottle of Champagne to christen *Water Pearl*, a 68-foot schooner on the island of Bequia.[5] It had been under construction for three years.[6] One of the boat's owners was Bob Dylan. Dylan had suggested the name Resurrection.

The boat's builder, Chris Bowman, was a Californian who spent a number of years after he left school on adventures around the world. His final adventure, before settling down, was rebuilding a boat for a man in Grenada. When the boat put to sea, Bowman says, it took on water and literally washed up on Bequia, lucky not to sink. As Bowman tells it,[7] Bequians have a tradition of wooden boat-building and are master sailors and seamen. For a time, he became part of that tradition.

The first boat Bowman built on Bequia was a 40-footer, the *Just Right*. Then, the classic friend-of-a-friend scenario played out. On a visit to California, Bowman met up with Ben, a childhood best friend. As kids, they played basketball at the home of sportswriter Jim Murray in Point Dume. And as it happened Bob Dylan had purchased Murray's house and additional surrounding property, a total of 17 acres, and was building his onion-domed mansion. Ben worked for Bob Gilbert one of the builders working on Dylan's house. Gilbert was interested in building a boat and had seen pictures, via Ben, of the 40-footer Bowman had built. Gilbert asked Bowman, all of 26, if he could build a 120-footer. Of course, being 26, Chris said, "sure." Somewhere down the line Dylan became a partner. When Gilbert soured on the project, Dylan and Bowman became co-owners and partners. The initial budget for the partners to split was $125,000.

The boat, which could sleep 12, was built of fine and exotic materials: greenheart, a wood from Guyanan jungles formed the keel and silver bali,

---

5 / Chris Bowman, Skype interview by the author, January 25, 2019. Perkins had the honorific "Godmother of the *Water Pearl*."

6 / Simmons, *Judy Boat Building*, Island Life Stories, April 1, 2018

7 / Chris Bowman published his own book in late 2019 called *Me, The Boat and a Guy Named Bob*. For the life of me, I can't figure out what that's about!

described as a 'light fragrant wood with worm resistant qualities', was used for the deck planks. A local sailmaker requisitioned one of the island's only two tennis courts for cutting 3,505 square feet of sails.

Once the craft was completed in June of 1980, the *Water Pearl* was available for charter at $500 per person, per week – mostly, but not always, when Dylan himself wasn't using it.[8] Rather than being Dylan's boat it was Dylan's investment in a boat with right of usage.

Dylan took many trips accompanied only by Bowman, the co-owner's wife, Vanessa, and infant daughter, Clara. To get to the boat, Dylan would usually fly in unaccompanied[9] from New York to St. Martin, where Bowman would pick him up and set sail from the harbor of either Phillipsburg or Marigot. Getting Dylan to come on board the boat the first time was not easy, according the Bowman. He remembers Dylan's first visit being in August or September 1980.[10] Dylan discovered that on the boat and the islands, he could relax, swim, and windsurf and not be recognized. He was relaxed and undemanding, one of the family. On his first trip, he didn't even bring a guitar, so Bowman borrowed an old cheap 5-string. After that, Dylan brought one of his instruments and often went to the stateroom to write and play.

Bowman remembers hearing reggae music being played all day on the boat. Dylan also listened to tapes he had brought by Hank Williams, Mickey and Sylvia and others. Dylan, at Bowman's suggestion, traveled ashore with the two West Indian crew members to see old black and white zombie and vampire films in a ramshackle theater. The Bequian crew, Cyril Stowe and Kingsley King – Bamu and Kingsley[11] – used the term "I and I" constantly and kept Bob Marley and Peter Tosh playing through the ship's speakers.[12]

8/ Brady, Tad "The Boats of Bequia," Cruising World, (Newport, RI, June 1981). Interview with Chris Bowman

9 / Clinton Heylin claims Dylan was frequently with Clydie King. Bowman says that the only time Dylan was not alone was once when his children were with him. Heylin, *Trouble in Mind*, 165. Interview with Chris Bowman

10 / Dylan began rehearsals for a Fall tour and songs for a new album on September 18, 1980, so this trip may include the St. Vincent locale where Dylan awoke from a dream and begin writing 'Caribbean Wind'11 / Christopher Bowman, e-mail, January 27, 2019

11 / Bamu and Kingsley were combined into one name on the Special Thanks inner sleeve for *Knocked Out Loaded*, an album seemingly not inspired by Island influences, rather by "it's time for another album."

Water Pearl sank off Panama in 1988, after failing a nighttime harbor entrance. One story is that *Water Pearl* had been sold to an Australian and was being sailed to the Pacific via the Canal. According to Chris Bowman in *Me, The Boat and a Guy Named Bob*, (Australia 2019) the crew was using an old chart which did not reflect then current guide lights. The boat foundered on a reef. When Bowman told Dylan, what happened (after Lloyds of London paid the insurance settlement), Bob responded, "Man, it's like that reef has been sitting there waiting for you since the very beginning."

Dylan told interviewers, and wrote in *Chronicles*, of sailing the Caribbean and stated that 'Jokerman' was written on one such outing. It has long been reported he visited singer-songwriter Bankie Banx, 'the Anguillan Bob Dylan', on Anguilla. Years later, on November 22, 1987, Dylan rehearsed one of Bankie's songs, 'Prince of Darkness', in a very early Never Ending Tour rehearsal with G. E. Smith. Banx' album version of the song dates to 1982, so this could tie in with Dylan's visit to Bankie in the period when the *Infidels* writing was taking place, most likely January 1983.

The islands, its stories and spirit pervade *Infidels*, and are the starting point for several songs and their atmosphere. Sly Dunbar and Robbie Shakespeare, Jamaican natives, provided the rhythm for the album.

There is one claim that the experience of sailing *Water Pearl* was not the sole fact influencing the spirit and sound. Larry Sloman, aka Ratso, remembers Dylan visiting him and asking who a good choice for producer for his next album would be. According to Sloman, he played Dylan records by Mark Knopfler and by Sly Dunbar and Robbie Shakespeare.[13]

Finally, in commenting to writer Paul Zollo about 'I & I', Dylan said, "That was one of them Caribbean songs. One year a bunch of songs just came to me hanging around down in the islands."[14]

Notebooks

Substantial notoriety has been attached to the notebooks Dylan used to work

---

12 / emails from Chris Bowman January 21 and 22, 2019

13 / Larry 'Ratso' Sloman, phone interview by the author, June 6, 2009

14 / Zollo, Paul. *Singers and Songwriters: Expanded Edition,* (New York: Da Capo Press 1997), 83

out the lyrics for *Blood on the Tracks*. His proclivity for using 3x5 inch spiral notebooks was alive and ticking during the 1982-1983 period. Two notebooks in the Dylan Archives evidence continued writing and a lot of travel between ports. One can almost imagine a remaining scent of sea air as St. Martin, St. Vincent, The Virgin Islands, Guadeloupe, St. Barts and Bermuda (for banking) are name-checked.[15] One notebook is protected by a tan cover, the other is coverless. It should be digitized soon, as even latex-gloved hands pose a threat to its survival.

The notebooks, like almost everything Dylan commits to paper, are undated. One exception: the first page of the tan notebook is marked 1/23/83. That was a Sunday. But as others have noted, something written on a notebook page, even the first page, does not mean it was written first or at any particular time.[16] This date may be accurate however. Chris Bowman says that he picked up Dylan in St. Martin on a Sunday in January. Two notebook pages later, Dylan wrote "Saturday-St. Bart's." That was evidently January 29. The next day, Bowman and Dylan watched the Washington Redskins defeat the Miami Dolphins in the Super Bowl while drinking rum at the Santa Fe Bar in St. Bart's.[17] Later Dylan wrote "Who won the Super Bowl," an ongoing taunt or exultation extending beyond the day of the game or, simply, a rum-induced lack of memory. Twenty-two of the 58 notebook pages are blank, but the rest reflect continued, if sporadic, composition.

Within a few days of Super Bowl Sunday, Dylan traded the constant mid-Eighties tropical warmth for 3 degrees F. He went to Duluth for boyhood friend Lou Kemp's wedding.[18]

In the notebook he apparently started January 23, Dylan appears to write down thoughts, concepts and verse as they come to mind. They are repeated, modified, shifted and shaped into song, or forgotten about, as time passes.

15/ To get flavor of working with these small notebooks, Anne Margaret Daniel's 'There Will Be Blood' article in the *2019 Hot Press Annual* cannot be commended more highly
16/ BDA: Notebook one is archived as 2016.01 B99 F01 The second notebook is 2016.01 B99 F03
17 / Interview with Chris Bowman
18 / Facebook posting by Lou Kemp
Confirmed by message from Kemp January 31, 2019. "He came to my wedding in- between those dates," i.e. St Bart's and meeting Mark Knopfler and Alan Clark in NYC

The first page on which words appear in a notebook do not mean that's when the song began. For example, on the sixth notebook page Dylan wrote "wished I'd been a doctor, maybe I'd-a saved a few lives that have been lost." So, it would seem this could be THE starting point? Not likely, for the January 23, 1983 date to be taken seriously as a starting point, we have to ignore a lyric draft containing the same lament of not practicing medicine and was actually dated "typed in the dark by flashlight 11/15/82." It's wise not to get too hung up on exact dates and exact order of the evolution. The development of the art was not linear. The mystery is that the thoughts get put together in a way that makes poetic and emotional and, often, logical sense.

Likely Dylan was already well on his way to developing many lyrics and songs. He was planning to record a new album of the songs he was working on and was considering a celebrity producer for the project. Beginning in Autumn 1982, reports of Dylan playing new songs for friends appeared in the fan information letter *The Wicked Messenger*. In January 1983, the British music paper *Melody Maker* reported that Dylan rang the entrance bell of Frank Zappa's house in Laurel Canyon and, after confirming his identity to a doubting Zappa, played him new songs, either with words, or without, depending on what report is believed, and discussed Frank's being a producer. A few weeks later, David Bowie's name was being floated, then Elvis Costello. And finally, or once again, the arrow spun and settled on Mark Knopfler. To sum up, something, like a new album, was in the works.

Words appear in the notebook almost as reminders to himself to think about what he wants to write. Or perhaps continue to work on. Madam (sic) Butterfly is on page two; Nightingale, on the third page, written like a title, but no hint of a joker man or anyone else dancing to the tune. We learn that "Philadelphia is a rough place, was almost as rough as Baltimore." Try to connect the dots on this: "Poland for breakfast, Beirut for dessert". And that's preceded by "Never could learn to drink blood and call it wine". Other scraps of 'Someone's Got a Hold of My Heart', Tell Me', 'Too Late/Foot of Pride' and 'Don't Fall Apart on Me Tonight' pop up once, and then show up a few pages later with one or two more lines.

There are repeated notebook pleas to a woman, or women, not to go away or, at least, to come back and experience the joy of reunion.

Advice is remembered: "be easy baby, ain't nothing worth stealing". Odd observations are jotted down: "The names of the dead are written in wine".

Other Infidels lines and thoughts scattered through the notebook include: "that old ship of Zion... dead lion... tell me I need to know... not for as long as he like... wild fire... storm... got to have done some worthless deed...land of permanent bliss... do the opposite of what the experts say... years since a strange woman slept in my bed... I took an untrodden path once...the streets are filled with vipers who've lost all ray of hope...".

There are full versions of verses and an almost complete embryonic working of 'I & I'. There are the first preliminary verses of 'Too Late', which morphed into 'Foot of Pride'. All of these come close to the end of the notebook. Then, after a half-dozen blank pages, there are stray observations, lyrics that have not developed, an address at Hunter College, a date noted next to the address for a Yeshiva in Brooklyn, phone numbers for recording industry associates. There are familiar names: Don DeVito, Bill Graham, Ratso, Ted Pearlman, Lynn Goldsmith, Danny Kortchmer, Mark Knopfler, Steve Ripley, Howard Shore and Jerry Scheff. This could indicate that on a pleasure trip, business was close at hand.

Finally, almost at the end of the notebook, following three blank pages, is this list:

Sweetheart
I & I
Death
License
Don't Fall

Joker
Neighbor
Julius
Tell Me
Man of Peace
Union

Thus, the first notebook appears to have a settling-in component, composition and then daily notations about details such as phone numbers and random reminders ("NordicTrack?") toward the end of the notebook. As I discuss individual songs in later chapters, I will refer to this notebook.

The second notebook does not indicate use for composing and is likely contemporaneous with the time of recording *Infidels* and the months after. Specific dates in May and July 1983 bear this out, if we can rely on written dates. Additionally, a date for a Pan Am flight appears. Dylan riffs on seeing a female comedian, apparently Joan Rivers from his 'can we talk' observation. He observes that human rights in America have evolved into pure license to visit all manner of harm and immorality upon others.

He defines himself as a "spiritual person" who gets hit with"a lot of inquiries", perhaps about the difference, if any, between a pagan and an atheist. In the second notebook, Dylan wrote further reflections on spiritual matters.[19]

After an early attempt at the post-Infidels song 'Straight A's in Love', here called 'You're Straight A', the second notebook takes a startling and seemingly direct (always remember it's Bob) discussion of the experience of turning to Jesus. In November 27, 1985, Dylan told Robert Hillburn, "I feel like pretty soon I am going to write about that," he said. "I feel like I got something to say but more than you can say in a few paragraphs in a newspaper." It appears he had already done so in this second notebook.

Following this notebook passage, Dylan wrote that once a person understands the nature of the world, he/she can see that since Adam and Eve mankind has furthered the success of evil. He reflected on short-term heroes and he noted that inventor Alexander Graham Bell was only great for a moment and no one "prays to him or confesses anything to him."[20]

Before we gallop to the finish line of understanding Dylan's pillars of belief, contemporaneously, when he was in New York, Dylan was attended classes at the Yeshiva of Flatbush, founded in 1927. He wrote a "Saturday 9:30 P.M." reminder in Notebook One.

---

19 / *Material in the Dylan Archives is available for research. The intellectual property rights are retained by Bob Dylan. When a project moves from research to publication, permission is required from the Archives and the rights holder. As a result of the process of securing permissions, some of Bob Dylan's writings may only be discussed in general terms for publication*
20 / *BDA Notebook one*

Infidels session engineer Neil Dorfsman remembered one rare bit of small talk when after a Yeshiva visit, Dylan commented on a health food store and "right next door was a flower shop." Not the most revelatory small talk.[21]

During this time, Dylan also had a relationship with Miriam and Meir Rhodes, who lived on President Street in Brooklyn. "Their Crown Heights home became a hub, drawing an eclectic mix of personalities. Bob Dylan, a Dylan childhood friend, and the Tzaddik of Leningrad (Izzy Kogan) were often at their Shabbos table."[22]

The Rhodes associated with the Chabad Lubavitch.[23] Chabad translates as "wisdom." Lubavitch is a Russian term representing "City of brotherly love." Chabad characterizes itself as a" philosophy, a movement and an organization."[24] Chabad's most visible programs are in education and were first seen in establishment of Jewish Day Schools. Dylan participated in Chabad telethons three times, beginning in 1986.

While the telethon appearances, complete with a Rebbe bestowing blessings on the abashed Dylan, speak for themselves as much as anything Dylan is involved in speaks on a single level, his commitment to a specific religion is irrelevant. "I never said I was born again," he claimed. When Robert Hillburn questioned him during an October 30, 1983 interview about a rumor that Dylan was recording for Mitzvah Records his response was, "You can say I'm planning to do 20 records for them. Say I'm going to do all my records from now on for them."

It appears that the notebook entries about the nature of the world and man were in Dylan's head as he wrote lyrics for what became Infidels. One can surmise that the world as it was given to Adam and Eve was perfect and unspoiled and because they did not follow, or believe, God's one commandment, they were deemed nonbelievers, as were their descendants. 'Man has invented his doom,' indeed. Dylan may believe he can survive the

21 / Neil Dorfsman phone Interview by author January 22, 2019

22 / During the weeks of the Infidels sessions, Dylan would study in Brooklyn, not for specific religious purpose, but to further his understanding
Interview with Josh Abbey February 5, 2019

23 / *Chabad Lubavitch News* January 24, 2019

24 / Chabad Lubavitch website

inevitable end man's infidelity brings to earth. But he cannot stop himself from commenting on the situation song by song:

'This Land Is Condemned' ('Blind Willie McTell')

'Tomorrow All Activity Will Cease' ('Man of Peace')

'Only A Matter of Time 'til Night Comes Stepping In' ('Jokerman')

'The World Could Come to An End Tonight' ('I and I')

'Man Has Invented His Doom' ('License to Kill')

'Your Time Will Come' ('Foot of Pride')

'This World Is Ruled by Violence' ('Union Sundown')

'The Cities Are on Fire with the Burning Flesh of Men' ('Death Is Not the End')

'A World That's Been Raped and Defiled' ('Lord Protect My Child')

'Running Out the Clock, Time Standing Still' ('Neighborhood Bully')

In the October *LA Times* interview conducted by Hillburn Dylan expanded on the views expressed in the notebooks: "To me, the greatest sinners were the shoddy lawyers, corrupt promoters, professional gossip peddlers—the wolves in sheep's clothing who present themselves as saints, but whose duty is to nobody but themselves. Reality is distorted when a sinner is presented as some dirty wino who sleeps in his clothes or some run-of-the-mill whore with two black eyes. It's easy to pull the wool down over somebody's eyes. Most people think Sylvester Stallone is a boxer."

Yet, because if these were a person's sole thoughts it would be difficult to get up each morning to see another day, Dylan answered a question about his outlook by responding in terms of his work. Asked if he is more pessimistic than in the Sixties, he replied: "I don't think any of my songs have been pessimistic. In every song I've written, I think, there has been a way out because that's just the nature of me."

Though the songs for *Infidels* were not complete, Dylan was far enough along to zero in on a date for recording. Mark Knopfler survived the producer sweepstakes. There would be an album recorded. When will work begin? Who would the musicians be?

2:

The Team Comes Together

Midday, on Friday, February 11, 1983, Alan Clark, the keyboard player for Dire Straits, got into a cab on Central Park West in Manhattan. On this crisp, clear day he headed south to Bank Street in New York's West Village where bandmate and guitar virtuoso, Mark Knopfler, had a brownstone residence. Clark, Knopfler and possibly engineer Neil Dorfsman, were to meet with Dylan to take a first look at the songs and chords that Dylan intended to begin recording six weeks or so later. By the time Dylan arrived in the late afternoon, a storm that would dump 17.5 inches of snow on New York[25] had begun. It is unclear whether Mick Taylor, whom Dylan had recruited the previous summer to play guitar on the album, was present. Drummer Sly Dunbar and bass player Robbie Shakespeare were not there.

Clark and Knopfler were playing pool in the lower level of the brownstone when Dylan arrived. According to Clark, he looked up and saw Dylan, standing at the top of the stairs and with the front door open behind him, seeming to be enveloped in a glow. "It seemed as if there could be angels singing behind him."[26]

Dire Straits had a tour break from late December 1982 until March 4, 1983, when they were due in Sydney, Australia. Their tour of Australia, New Zealand and Japan in support of the Love Over Gold album was to conclude April 5. Dylan's recording sessions were arranged for the Power Station Studio in Manhattan, possibly with the help of Dire Straits manager Ed Bicknell, and would begin on April 11. The session work had to conclude or at least pause by May 5, to allow Dire Straits to open a two-month European tour in Hamburg, Germany, May 11.

During the post-December tour break, Knopfler returned home one January afternoon and was told some odd news by his then-wife Lourdes. Dylan, whom she may not have even recognized, simply showed up at their door looking for Mark. After waiting for a while and having a cup of tea, Bob left, phoned Mark later and asked him to produce his next record. The request was specifically to produce, with Knopfler's guitar probably being assumed but not spelled out.[27] Before Knopfler was recruited, Dylan had considered other celebrity musicians as producer.

There were reports of a similar unannounced visit in December to Frank

25 / Alan Clark, phone interview with the author, November 5, 2018
26 / Interview with Alan Clark
27 / emails from Ed Bicknell, Dire Straits and Knopfler's then manager. January 26-28, 2019

Zappa at his Laurel Canyon house. Zappa talked a lot to the press about this, which probably eliminated him quickly, as did his reputation as a control freak.[28] In one of Frank's blabathons, he said Dylan played him 14 songs—just melodies. Zappa went on that he asked Dylan, "This material doesn't have the "Big J[esus]" in it, does it, Bob?"

"No Frank," Dylan supposedly responded. It's such a good story, it almost doesn't have to be true.[29]

Others said to be in consideration for producer, but less talkative, were David Bowie, Steve Winwood, and Elvis Costello. According to those familiar with the goings-on, it was Dylan's idea to get this level of help, saying at one point to Knopfler that his previous releases were 'home records'. This should have been of interest to Jerry Wexler, producer of the Grammy-winning 'Gotta Serve Somebody' on *Slow Train Coming*.

Over the previous year, Knopfler had attained a level of recognition bordering on reverence for his distinctive guitar playing, as well as his songwriting and unique singing. Being famous has its pressures but becoming even more famous ramps up the pressure exponentially. Knopfler came into producing Bob Dylan while dealing with the increased burden of that mantle.

Turning back to the February 11 events at Bank Street, according to Clark, they rehearsed songs intended for the album, and they were all "Bob Dylan tunes." During the afternoon, the three musicians also played pool and Dylan talked about his boat.

By the time they reconvened in April, although the songs were the same they had heard in February, many of the melodies, rhythms and words had changed. And they would continue to do so even to the last day Knopfler and Clark recorded on May 5. And more changes occurred after they had departed.

Between Bank Street in February and April 11 at the Power Station studio, there were no rehearsals or rough tapes to review.[30] There was also

28 / Interview with Chris Bowman
29 / Blitz Magazine April 1983, quoted in The Wicked Messenger April 24, 1983
30 / Interview with Alan Clark
Robbie Shakespeare, FaceTime interview with author, January 15, 2019
Sly Dunbar, FaceTime interview with author January 19, 2019
Interview with Neil Dorfsman January 22, 2019

a discernible lack of cohesion during the sessions. No one has described animosity and, all tapes reflect relaxed professionalism, but these were five great musicians who had never recorded together as a unit.

Essentially, there were three camps, non-warring, but with their separate comfort levels: Bob and Mick Taylor; Mark, Alan, and engineer Neil Dorfsman; and Sly and Robbie.[31] At the very least, they did not know each other's moves instinctively, as would a group that had been together for years. And other than Sly and Robbie, they did not have rich experience of being studio musicians other than for their groups. Finally, Knopfler was the only one who had previously been in the studio with Dylan, on the *Slow Train Coming* sessions four years prior. In sum, it was an unusual dynamic, added to by Dylan's natural contrarian tendencies to 'upset the apple cart', according to Dorfsman, "There just never seemed to be a complete meeting of the minds. Now, those differences of energy happen on a lot of recordings, but it never quite got sorted out in this case."

Sly Dunbar, though, remembers it going smoothly, "...wish all sessions could be like that. No superstars." He found Dylan very cool and relaxed, but Sly did say that between Mark and Bob he didn't know who was the producer.[32]

While Knopfler was chosen to be the producer, the responsibility for details such as arranging hotels, transportation, meals and booking studio time fell to others. Some of the nitty-gritty work went to Ed Bicknell, who was the manager for Dire Straits. "I wanted to make sure that Mark and Alan were going to have sufficient time to complete [their work] and not end up exhausted when the European leg started," Bicknell said. "I recall sitting with a calendar and counting up free weeks and then figuring in travel, allowing for jet lag, the kind of thing people like me do. Plus how long to make the sessions, how many hours a day, how many days a week, start times, type of toilet paper, plastic cups versus china, are pets allowed, dress code, what type of mineral water, and are Sly and Robbie vegans,[33] is anybody else vegan?" Bicknell thought he needed Dylan's input but did not speak directly to him. "I

31 / Interview with Neil Dorfsman
32 / Interview with Sly Dunbar via FaceTime January 19, 2019.
33 / One story is that Sly and Robbie stayed at the Howard Johnson's on 10th Avenue because they liked the fried fish.

spoke to the driver," Bicknell recalls, "and the driver spoke to Bob." The driver was likely Gary Shafner,[34] Dylan's personal assistant at the time.

Bicknell's efforts came when he was heavily engaged in ensuring a success for the upcoming Straits tour of Australia, New Zealand and Japan in March and early April and a May to July European tour. And, suddenly, here's the Dylan album matter. Left for later was Mark's producer contract: "As usual, contracts came after the event," according to Bicknell. For the actual sessions, Bicknell coordinated with Don DeVito, head of A&R for Columbia, and put together a rough budget. Columbia Records paid the various 'component' expenses.

With the logistical matters having been, and continuing to be handled by others, the musicians convened at The Power Station at 441 West 53rd Street at around 1p.m. on April 11, 1983. The building in Hell's Kitchen,[35] was once the studio for the *Let's Make a Deal* television game show (check out the Steve Goodman song 'Door Number Three') and had been built as an electrical relay station for Consolidated Edison.

The building was converted into a recording studio by Tony Bongiovi and Bob Walters in 1977. The 33,000-square-foot facility's oversized live-sounding rooms became the choice for many artists in the Seventies and Eighties. These including Diana Ross (Diana), Gary U.S. Bonds (Dedication), Bruce Springsteen (The River) and Dire Straits (Love Over Gold). The Gary U.S. Bonds album included Dylan's 'From A Buick Six'. Neil Dorfsman had an engineering role on all these records. Dylan admired Love Over Gold.[36]

Ironically, the experience Knopfler and Dorfsman had recording *Love Over Gold* influenced the technology chosen for recording *Infidels*. The Dire Straits album had been recorded as albums were in 1982, on analog tape. Dorfsman thought that despite techniques used to guard against it, analog modifies the sound being recorded when it is played back over time and, in fact, degrades sound with each pass. Whether it was a nearly imperceptible phenomenon or actual, it was real to Dorfsman and Knopfler. Each thought that on the song 'Private Investigations', the

34 / email from Ed Bicknell
35 / No evidence of Alicia Keys from that time
36 / Interview with Neil Dorfsman

piano sound degraded with every successive play. They vowed never to use analog again,[37] perhaps a vow not made in a vacuum, as they knew that digital recording machines had recently been introduced.

The first commercially available digital recorders became available in the late Seventies. At least three competing technologies hit the market: Sony's Dash, Mitsubishi's ProDigi and a 3M system. In a story that plays out again and again in the electronics industry, each of the formats was incompatible with the others. The digital information – a series of 0s and 1s – was laid on tape in different patterns depending on the manufacturer, and the tape itself differed in width. Tape for the 3M system was 1 inch and would accommodate 32 minutes of multi-track recording. Mitsubishi tape was also 1 inch, but not compatible. Sony Dash tape was one-half inch. This created a format fight to the death in a very small niche: professional recording. Such was the infancy of digital recording that tape was used. Now the signal goes direct to a hard drive.

In what must be presumed to be a pure and delicious coincidence, the first studio to install the 3M system was Sound 80 in Minneapolis where Dylan famously re-recorded several songs in December 1974 before releasing *Blood on the Tracks*. The studio also produced the first commercially released digital recording, featuring the St. Paul Chamber Orchestra.

The 3M system brought into the Power Station was an upgrade from the initial models in that it could record 32 tracks. There were not many of these machines in the world then, and it's not precisely known how many, if any, survive today. The scarcity and expense meant that the main machine was the only machine. Because of this and the $90 cost of each reel of tape, engineers only hit record on the 3M machine when it seemed Dylan was actually ready to go.

Nothing was slated; no one announced a la Producer Bob Johnston during the *Blonde on Blonde* sessions, "'I Want You' - take three." Not until the second week of the sessions were there continually running analog tapes, referred to in some instances as library or backup tapes. In the

37 / Ibid

Infidels sessions, they were documented as 'Run Tapes'.[38]

Dylan brought Mick Taylor into the mix of musicians for the recording session. Since resigning from the Rolling Stones in 1974, Taylor had kept busy playing with a wide assortment of people, including John Phillips, Alvin Lee, Little Feet, Jack Bruce and Bruce Gary. In 1982, he was with John Mayall, Colin Allen and John McVie which is when Dylan reportedly caught a summer show in Los Angeles and talked with Taylor about recording together. Or Dylan had visited a recording session where Taylor, Bruce, and Gary were working. Or he had recorded songs with the three. Whatever the real story, Dylan liked Taylor's playing and had him in mind for something, someday. And now, here he was in the studio string-to-string with Mark Knopfler. The question of how two strong lead guitar players were going to mesh was of less than secondary importance to Dylan. Throughout his career he had a mad scientist approach for seeing what happens when mixing disparate ingredients in a studio or on stage. And, perhaps, Dylan had some concern that if the musicians were all from Dire Straits, it would sound like a Dire Straits album with Bob doing the vocals. If that were the case, it made sense for Dylan to make his own choices for some of the other players.

The rhythm section was also Dylan's choice. Sly Dunbar and Robbie Shakespeare were native to Jamaica and had played together since 1972. They had played for many artists and on albums with which Dylan was familiar, particularly Peter Tosh and Jimmy Cliff. Dunbar and Shakespeare had become, justifiably, the go-to rhythm section. Neither Sly nor Robbie – it's tempting to just say or write slyandrobbie – recall having met Bob before being asked by an intermediary to play on the sessions that became Infidels. Perhaps Bankie Banx had planted the seed.[39] Robbie recalls being contacted in Nassau and being told Dylan wanted to work with him in the studio. "Without hesitation, I said 'Yes,'" Shakespeare said.

38 / In the early stages of research, there was confusion whether archival analog library tapes existed. Fortunately, some of the participants remembered such recordings. This encouraged a deeper look. Documents were uncovered that helped identify the tapes which were located and used to enhance this book

39 / Interview with Larry 'Ratso' Sloman. According to Sloman, he had played Dylan a Sly and Robbie album when the singer came to his apartment seeking suggestions on producers and musicians for the forthcoming sessions

CHAPTER 2 / THE TEAM COMES TOGETHER

3:

The Setup

Between the February Bank Street get together with Knopfler, Clark and Dorfsman and the beginning of recording in April, Dylan spent more time on Water Pearl.[40] By April 3, he was back in Los Angeles and boarding a flight to New York. This date is confirmed by Gary Aloian and Bob Scott, a paparazzi team, who were staked out at LAX and claimed they got in a scuffle with Bob that day.[41]

Planning for the sessions was complete; the studio was booked. One hopes the proper mineral waters were stocked and at the ready. Engineer Dorfsman and assistant engineer Josh Abbey, were ready to hit the record button on the 3M digital console. The six musicians took their places in the wood-panelled room with its high-peaked ceiling. Inside the air-conditioned studio, they were a world apart from the spring weather that was warming from the 57 degrees of the initial recording day to the mid-Eighties of the final week. It may be snarky to note, but on April 22, when Dylan had labored on ten attempts of 'Too Late',[42] he laid down a couple of verses of 'Dark as a Dungeon'.

In the room were an assortment of very talented and different personalities. Robbie Shakespeare and Sly Dunbar were laid-back Jamaicans. Sly was unruffled and not intimidated by being with one of ther era's greatest artists. When the others went into the control room to listen to playbacks, Dunbar would stay at his drum kit reading heavy metal magazines.[43]

Mick Taylor, who made periodic attempts at being a frontman in a career of otherwise being a tremendous sideman, was relatively unassertive. Taylor had resigned from the Rolling Stones primarily because he feared being subsumed by the lifestyle. Mick had already experienced the sudden ascent to great fame that Knopfler was then experiencing. Maybe he was content to be at a place in his life where striving for the top was not as important as it had been. There is reasonable debate whether Knopfler was pleased with Taylor's presence, but the natural competition you would expect possibly

40 / Chris Bowman, Email, February 5, 2019
41 / UPI Archives, May 20, 1983
Prosecutors declined prosecution of Dylan, saying "Aloian had it coming."
42 / 'Too Late' underwent a metamorphosis into 'Foot of Pride' four days later
43 / Interview with Neil Dorfsman

contributed to great performances from both.

Mark Knopfler and Alan Clark shared history as bandmates and were fitting in this work between tour commitments. Perhaps it was a labor of love, but it was also labor that required putting everything they had been and would be doing on hold for five weeks, mentally and emotionally. And in Dylan they were working with an unmatched talent, and a person "incredibly, easily bored" and not naturally comfortable to laboring on a track. And if finding the heart of the song took time, Dylan was not averse to playing mind games to keep the dynamic from becoming stagnant. No one was at anyone's throat. It simply was not the usual way for these men to work. Stirring the pot was Bob Dylan. He is a one-of-a-kind artist, comfortable with letting a song develop around him as opposed to saying "This is how it's going to go. You do this, you do that..." On some days, the group spent an entire day on many takes of just one or two songs. Other days seem to have been wasted in doodling, noodling, grooving and spending a minute or two on covers. Dylan constantly rewrote and revised during downtime. Some of the unproductive days might have thus been filled. While Dylan was writing, musicians and crew stood around or jammed.

There were seventeen days when recordings were produced and logged. On six of those days, most of the recorded material was essentially random playing, Dylan melodies without words or a verse or two of a cover song, such as 'Lover's Concerto', 'Green Onions', or 'The Harder They Come'. Such fooling around certainly isn't limited to Dylan. Most, if not all, musicians do it to release tension or find a spark that leads to where they want to go. That's part of the fun of being in a studio with other musicians. It is, after all, called playing music. On the other hand, studio time is costly and the clock was ticking. The Straits contingent would only be available until May 5.

Knopfler, as described by Ed Bicknell, would not have been ruffled by these side roads. "Mark gets on with things, is disciplined without being overly dictatorial, is always on time and ready to go. He definitely has the view that recording should be fun."[44]

Mid-way through April, it appears, pressure came not from the walls of the

---

44 / email from Ed Bicknell

Power Station or Knopfler's developing fame. Bicknell remembers receiving an unexpected and unannounced call from promoter/manager Bill Graham. Graham's business relationship with Dylan dated to 1973, when he put together the Dylan/Band 1974 return to touring.[45] "You never forget a call from Bill Graham," Bicknell said. Although Dylan was not under management at the time, Graham asked if Bicknell "could prevail on Mark to 'speed things up.'" Graham was quite insistent, and to this day Bicknell is unclear whether the pressure came from Graham on behalf of the record label, or Graham himself. Whatever the reason, Knopfler was "bemused" by the situation, but even if he wanted to accede to the request – which he didn't do – Bob set the pace of recording. Bicknell doubted that Dylan was susceptible to this kind of corporate pressure; and in the end, despite subsequent weekly hassling calls from Graham, Bicknell and Knopfler ignored that pressure.

Unfortunately, Graham is not alive to provide his side of the story, but it would doubtless have been colorful, as he is remembered as referring to Dylan as "that motherfucker we're dealing with," affectionate talk in Graham-speak. At some point in the process, certainly by the time the mixing was underway, Graham quit calling. Rather, he became a presence at the Power Station.[46] Josh Abbey, who was assistant engineer from the first session until the final mix says he would have known if Knopfler was affected by Graham's interference during his time as the nominal producer.[47]

Record companies work six months in advance on their release schedule, and, from contemporaneous reports, Columbia was telling sales representatives that a new Dylan album would be out in June or July. That was not going to happen. The previous album, *Shot of Love* was caught up in an endless cycle of re-recording and remixing into June 1981, the same

---

45 / Graham was circulating around Dylan's periphery at least dating to 1965. He can be seen in the audience in the recording of the December 5, 1965, press conference Dylan gave at San Francisco's KQED-TV. Graham had also given Dylan a poster of a concert he was promoting
46 / Interview with Josh Abbey, February 5, 2019. During this time, Graham, in full "sell" mode, made repeated attempts to get a squirming Dylan to endorse Senatorial Candidate Tom Hayden. Dylan kept declining and finally said, "Well, he's got a pretty nice wife(Jane Fonda)," and that was the end of the conversation
47 / Ibid

month Dylan was going on tour – presumably in support of a record that wasn't out. When *Shot of Love* was released August 10, 1981 in the U.S., the marketing support was scattered at best. The European tour was over, and a U.S. tour was two months away. Building any kind of sales momentum in such a situation was difficult, and, two years later Columbia did not want to repeat the experience.

A fall release for the new Dylan 1983 album would come when people were back at school or work. A later release would benefit from a holiday selling season. So perhaps the pressure wasn't coming from Columbia. These scenarios are well and good, but release dates are artificial targets in the first place. "Every album is late and over budget," according to assistant engineer Josh Abbey.[48]

Another possibility, and this is all conjecture, is that Dylan was reconsidering his one-month commitment to recording and having second thoughts. Dylan has a history of not confronting people directly. If he had second thoughts, he could have been asking himself whom he could get to be the bad guy. Bill Graham, with whom Dylan had a history, would be a perfect bad cop in this situation. To reiterate, Dylan was without management when the year began.

Don DeVito at Columbia could have always called Ed Bicknell directly, or Knopfler directly. Why midway through recording does Graham begin applying pressure? One of the functions of management is to do things the artist doesn't want to do. Once Knopfler left to tour Europe, the phone calls ceased. When Bicknell saw Graham later that summer at a Dire Straits concert, Graham said he was now Dylan's manager.

Whether Graham served merely as a tour promoter or full manager, Bicknell never knew.[49] No evidence supports the claim that Graham was formally engaged for anything other than tour promotion. Over the years, Dylan employed Jerry Weintraub and Elliot Roberts in similar capacities, putting together and managing tours.

For the recording of *Infidels*, the engineers chose to physically separate the musicians in the studio.

---

48 / Ibid.
49 / email from Ed Bicknell

Sly Dunbar had his drums in a room that had been 'the piano room'. Knopfler and Shakespeare were in a separate room. Mick Taylor began in the main room, with Dylan and keyboardist Clark, but soon moved to be near the amps.

Everyone could see Bob, but the setup necessitated everyone, including Dylan, use headphones. There was nothing out of the ordinary about this setup, other than negating a myth that Dylan eschewed headphones when recording.

At times, Dylan thought about using different instruments on the recordings. At one point, he suggested that he wanted to try playing a Farfisa keyboard on every track. On another day, he went into the studio next door to Studio C, and found Kurtis Blow recording. When he returned, he asked Dorfsman, "Hey Neil, can we make our drums sound like Kurtis' drums?" Dorfsman remembers thinking that he was doing everything to make a really good-sounding record, and now Bob wanted to use a Linndrum, which was an early drum machine. The Linndrum was "good for its time" when it was introduced in 1982, but it still was a drum machine.[50] Dylan could have been testing his team to see how they would react, or he could have had a passing interest.

Ironically, when on July 5, Dylan gave his only pre-release interview to Minnesotan Martin Keller, he discussed how music had changed. "Actually, it has become soulless and commercial. Lot of it is played with drum machines and synthesizers. Personally, I'd rather hear an orchestra and a real drummer. Machines don't have the depth of the human heart. There just isn't anyone home."[51] He repeated a similar thought in an interview with Robert Hillburn on June 13 1984.[52]

With a year (or a month in the Hillburn case) to think about the value of artificial drums, Dylan did knock on the door of machines. On July 26, 1984, fresh off a European tour, he went into Delta Sound in New York with Ron Wood, Anton Fig and possibly others and used what sounds suspiciously like a drum machine and definitely a synthesizer on 'Driftin' Too Far from Shore'. The ensuing recording sessions for *Empire Burlesque* had synthesizer tracks

50 / Interview with Neil Dorfsman
51 / Martin Keller Minneapolis City Paper. Version published in New Musical Express August 6, 1983
52 / Robert Hillburn (*Los Angeles Times*, August 5, 1984)

and drum machines on several songs.

The fact that Bob was using headphones while recording *Infidels* allowed the engineers to resolve a potential problem. For a portion of the album, Dylan played piano. Both engineers, Dorfsman and Abbey, call Dylan a 'great' piano player. When not on the piano, Dylan, who simply loves to play, was on guitar. And when playing guitar, he cranked up his amp, which was next to the piano, to a fairly high level. This arrangement would have prevented a clean keyboard recording. So, the following subterfuge was put into action: When it seemed that a take was likely, Dorfsman would dim the studio lights. Then, Josh Abbey would sneak into the studio, and put Dylan's amplifier on standby which muted the sound to the room. Dorfsman then fed the signal for the guitar to Bob's headphones. So Bob was happy, the piano could be recorded properly, and Dylan was none the wiser. Dylan eventually complained to Dorfsman, "Neil, my guitar sounds like a banjo in my headphones."

"I'll look into that Bob," said Neil.[53] Both Dorfsman and Abbey had a feeling that Dylan was amused that they thought they were putting one over on him. "He had a twinkle in his eye when he saw me in the room," said Abbey.

Another trick occurred when during a playback, Dylan said, "I want you to erase that part." Knopfler, who evidently did not agree, nudged Dorfsman who indeed kept the part on the recording. A few days later, when that section came up, Bob said, "I thought I told you to erase that. Why didn't you erase it?" Not wanting to throw Mark under the bus, Neil responded, "I dunno." Dylan considered and replied, "Good answer."[54]

One day, the musicians gathered in the control room to listen to what they'd just recorded, all except Dunbar who stayed at his drums with his magazines. And Dylan. Someone in the control room had just asked Shakespeare how he got the great sound on his bass. "Never change the strings, man," answered Robbie. At that moment, to everyone's horror, they witnessed Dylan out in the main room playing Robbie's bass. And breaking a string. "No worry, man,

53 / Interview with Neil Dorfsman
54 / Ibid

I've got a cigar box full of old strings," Shakespeare assured everyone.[55]

While Knopfler intended the sessions to be fun, some of the involved thought that the tension in the room made the month of recording needlessly serious. "One thing that was missing for me in making *Infidels*," says Abbey, "was laughter."

The Power Station Studio C was a state-of-the-art facility. According to Abbey, the SSL with Automation allowed overdubs and lyric punch-ins in a way Dylan would not have had previously. Muscle Shoals, where he had recorded in 1979 and 1980, did not have the technology. Cherokee in Los Angeles did not. In fact most of the LA studios did not have SSL with Automation until the late Eighties.[56] The equipment's expense, starting at $500,000, likely factored into this, but the excuse at the time from the non-adapters was the sound was too clean, "too perfect."[57]

This is the background for how Dylan purportedly discovered he did not have to re-record an entire song to change a word or a line. Dylan was working on 'I & I' (where there was a lyric change in the fourth verse, substituting four words for five, from the supposedly final version. "You mean I don't have to (sing the whole song)?" Dylan asked. "How would we do that? If I don't sing it again, don't we erase what's already there?" Abbey showed him how the computerized switch worked.

So Dylan went in and sang the line (probably 'Smokin' down the track'). Dylan came back into the control room and heard the original and the punch in, watched the lights going back and forth on the console. Dylan took it in, with his hand on his chin, nodded and said, "Pretty sneaky."

Since Dylan does not appear to have recorded in a studio before with this level of equipment, the reaction might not be a case of Dylan leg-pulling or game playing. This marked the start of the vocal changes that are found on the final album.[58]

What may be an example of game playing, or sheer eccentric isolation

---

55 / Ibid
56 / Slow Train Coming' and Saved were recorded in Muscle Shoals. Shot of Love was recorded in 1981 at a variety of Los Angeles studios
57 / Interview with Josh Abbey, February 9, 2019
58 / Ibid

from the surrounding world, is a story Abbey relates about footwear.[59] The mixing process continued into an extremely hot stretch of June weather in Manhattan, with temperatures hitting 90 degrees. Most days, Dylan, by himself, walked the eight blocks between his lodgings at The Ritz Carlton Hotel on Central Park South and the Power Station on West 53rd Street and 10th Avenue. As was his custom, Dylan wore heavy motorcycle boots. One scorching day, he accepted a ride with Abbey. When they got to the studio, Bob looked at Josh's Puma sneakers and asked "What do you call those?"

"These?"

"Yeah, what do you call those?" "These are Pumas."

"Where do you get those?"

"There are a half-dozen stores near your hotel that are pretty much devoted to sneakers."

When Dylan came in the next day, before Abbey could ask, Bob came over to him and said, "Do you know there are a million kinds of sneakers? They got sneakers for running, they got sneakers for jogging, they got sneakers for tennis, they got sneakers for basketball, they got sneakers for housewives vacuuming the floor. The guy asked me what I wanted them for. I told him I don't know. So I left, I didn't know what I wanted them for."

Abbey sensed that Dylan felt bad that he didn't have an answer for the salesman, who had spent an hour describing the differences but just wound up confusing his customer. Abbey suggested going back and telling the salesman that he just wanted something cool and comfortable to walk around in, to wear every day all day if he felt like it. The next day, Dylan came

---

59 / *Uncut*, "Recording With Bob Dylan: Chris Shaw Tells All", (London, October 27, 2008), Dylan brought out his wide-eyed studio naïf in 2006 when recording *Modern Times*. Engineer Chris Shaw, who had worked with Dylan on *Love And Theft* where they were physically cutting tape for 'Highwater', related in a June 2015 issue of *Uncut*, about getting Dylan to accept digital: "Actually it wasn't difficult to get him to go for using that. Between *Love and Theft* and *Modern Times*, we did a couple of film soundtrack things. When we did 'Cross The Green Mountain'...I said, 'Y'know, since this is just a one-off, it's not for an album I wouldn't mind trying Pro Tools, just so I can show you the benefits.' He said, 'Okay, whatever.' We did a take, and he was like, 'Okay, I want to edit out the second verse and put the fourth verse in there.' By the time he walked into the control room from the studio, I had it done. His eyes opened wise. 'You can edit that fast?' 'Yeah.' 'And you can keep everything?' You could just see the gears in his head suddenly spinning."

smiling into the studio. "I looked down," Abbey says, "and he's wearing the brightest white woven nylon shiny things with a black bottom. They were shoes designed for playing sports on Astroturf. He wore them for a couple of days; but as soon as the weather got cool enough, he was back wearing the motorcycle boots."[60]

As of the end of formal recording on May 2, 18 prospective songs had been recorded, 16 of which were Dylan originals. The album would include: 'Jokerman', Sweetheart Like You, 'Neighborhood Bully,' 'I & I', 'Man of Peace', 'Union Sundown', 'License to Kill', and 'Don't Fall Apart on Me Tonight'. The Dylan songs set aside were 'Blind Willie McTell', 'Tell Me', 'Someone's Got A Hold of My Heart', 'Foot of Pride', 'Death Is Not the End', 'Lord Protect My Child' and 'Julius and Ethel'. All but the last song was released either on a subsequent album or a Bootleg Series release. 'Angel Flying Too Close to the Ground', written by Willie Nelson, was released as a B side to four different singles released in international markets. 'This Was My Love' was written by James Herbert and recorded originally by Frank Sinatra in 1959. The Dylan recording of the song remains unreleased.

Overdub sessions began on May 8, three days after Knopfler and Clark had finished their work and departed, along with Dorfsman. According to Abbey, who drove Knopfler to the airport, the guitarist was not in a good mood. Mark had been adding not parts, per se, but "atmospheric fills", perhaps originally intending to put in more complete parts at a later date, but that was not to occur. (During the sessions, perhaps a glimpse into Knopfler's mood was caught by Abbey. "Mark sat and played Mick's part, over and over. I'm not certain what was going through his head, but he was playing with a vengeance, as if he was trying to prove something.")

The first day of overdubs percussionist Sammy Figueroa came in to work on four tracks.

On the 10th, Mick Taylor added potential licks to three tracks. A week later, horn players Bob Funk, Larry Etkin and Mark Rivera added parts to an ultimately unused overdub version of 'Neighborhood Bully'. Also in the studio on May 17 was Rolling Stones guitarist Ron Wood, who for whatever reason was not able to successfully contribute.[61] A group of CBS executives stood in the control room and watched the failed effort in stony silence, arms folded across their chests. Also watching was Dylan, leaning against the wall, his forehead pressed against his arm.[62]

On May 18, a more productive overdub session took place with members of the Full Force hip hop group providing vocals on outtakes of 'Death Is Not the End' and 'Tell Me'. Both of these songs were released years after the Infidels album,[63] although on at least one list in a Dylan notebook, both were potential candidates for the album, along with 'Julius and Ethel'.[64] As was the case in those days, once word of the album itself was in the wind, rumors began that an additional track or tracks, such as 'Death Is Not the End' would be on the cassette version. Research has not shown any consideration in the potential track lineups for 'Blind Willie McTell' or 'Foot of Pride'. According to Dorfsman, "Everyone was in shock when he dropped it ['Blind Willie McTell']." That shock remains today for everyone I interviewed.

The culling of tracks appears to have begun in earnest after May 10, when 'Clean Cut Kid' was worked on for the only time other than during the sessions.

'Lord Protect My Child' was set aside after May 15. 'Foot of Pride' went by the board after May 17. Full Force came in to add their vocals to the previously noted 'Death is Not the End' and 'Tell Me' on May 18, and that was that for those songs. No post-session work on 'Blind Willie McTell' is evident.

After Knopfler and Dorfsman left after the May 5 session, Josh Abbey was responsible for engineering. On June 4, Ian Taylor, an Australian producer, took command of the mixing process, and Abbey remained to assist. 'Angel Flying Too Close to the Ground' was worked on that day, so was still being tweaked at that moment.[65]

---

61 / The horns and Wood's guitar can be heard on a recording in the BDA.

62 / Josh Abbey interview

63 / 'Death Is Not the End' was on 1988s *Down in the Groove*

Tell Me was on 1991s *The Bootleg Series 1-3: Rare and Unreleased*

64 / BDA, Dylan notebook 1

65 / The preceding four paragraphs derive from information provided by the Dylan Archives as '*Infidels* Tape Notes'

Which tracks were chosen was partially 'artist choice' and partially technical. Beginning just after *Infidels*, CDs began to be the preferred format for selling music. A compact disc held 80 minutes of material. The groove technology of vinyl records limited the ideal length of a side to less than 24 minutes, 48 for a two-sided record. Any length beyond that, even with the skills of a mastering engineer, pushed the reproduction to unacceptable limits. *Infidels* as released timed at just under 52 minutes. The ultimately non-executed idea of adding a track to a cassette version would have been no problem, as the limit on those was up to 45 minutes per side. It does not appear that there was discussion of a double album, and it is appropriate to speculate about marketing considerations. Today, downloading is the preferred method for purchasing music, as opposed to streaming. Downloaded albums do not have any length limitations. Thus, the decisions that confronted the team in 1983 would not be a factor today. And, with the renewed popularity of the vinyl format, companies seem to have little problem releasing products—new and archival—as double albums.

When Dylan gave his July 5 interview to Martin Keller, he noted that the album was sequenced and ready to be slipped into a sleeve and shipped out. But the album was still untitled, and 'Angel Flying Too Close to the Ground' was still under consideration, according to Keller.

The *Infidels* sleeve credits Dylan and Knopfler as producers, Neil Dorfsman recorder, Josh Abbey as engineer, and Mixed and Remixed by Ian Taylor. Before these credits were finalized, Dylan hand wrote a draft and sketched a rough layout on a Ritz Carlton telephone message pad.[66] This postdates July 5, as Ian Taylor is given credit for the final mixes, except for 'License to Kill' which is credited to Dorfsman. Also, 'Angel Flying Too Close to the Ground' is not included.

At the top on one side is written "'FLESH - ZONE'; – 'FLASH - OF THE FLESH'". On the facing side, 'DECADENCE AND CHARM'.

The title of the album was *Surviving in a Ruthless World*, what Dylan had wanted to call it. "But someone pointed out to me that the last bunch of

66 / In the discussion of written lyrics in a later chapter, may of the drafts are on this same note paper. Josh Abbey stated that Dylan stayed at the Ritz during the sessions

albums I'd made all started with the letter "s". So I said 'Well, I don't wanna get bogged down in the letters.' And then infidels came into my head one day. I don't know what it means, or anything."[67] A quote delivered by Charlie Chaplin, famous for slapstick and later melancholy comedy, may or may not be an influencer of the original title: "This is a ruthless world and one must be ruthless to cope with it."[68] In Chaplin's *My Autobiography*, and other remarks throughout his life, one could construct a library of lines Dylan may have worked with.

Dylan's draft required editing if it was to be used as the template for the credits. Clark is spelled Clarke; Neil Dorfsman is Ian Dorfsman, Josh Abbey is merely Josh, Sweetheart is Sweethert, and Dylan at one point is Dyaln. The song order is slightly different with 'I & I' closing the first side rather than 'License to Kill'. 'I & I' became the third song on the second side on the released version, swapping spots with 'License' from Dylan's order. The thanks to those who "inspired or helped" are plentiful in the draft but not present on the released album.

Knopfler gets special thanks twice, along with Don DeVito.

The Knopfler special thanks were echoed by Dylan in the Martin Keller July 5 interview. "This is the easiest record I ever made because of Mark," Dylan said. "He understood the songs so well. Of course he's a songwriter himself, you know, and one of the most sensitive guitar players around. He encouraged me to go to the studio when I didn't feel like it, when I'd rather have been someplace else. Actually, we are soul mates. As far as guitar playing goes, he never steps all over with fancy licks. Yeah, Mark was incredible. He helped make this record in a thousand ways, not only musically, which in itself would have been enough. Brilliant guy, I can't say enough about him."[69]

On the bottom of the Ritz note pad, Dylan suggested phrases to possibly provide a feel for the album: "SPIRIT ROMP ZONE OF FLESH & BONE." "BLADE TO THE HEAT BALLADS & BLUES of Hip WhityBoy & Buffalo Woman."[70]

---

67 / Bob Dylan to Kurt Loder, March 1984, printed in *Rolling Stone* June 21, 1984
68 / From a scene in 1947's *Monsieur Verdoux*. Written and directed by Chaplin
69 / Martin Keller Interview
70 / BDAA, 2016.01 B36 F07 01

When the album was finally "slipped in the sleeve," as Dylan put it to Keller, the credits, which were placed on an inner sleeve, were significantly pared down to straight-forward recognition.

Infidels was released on vinyl and cassette on October 27, 1983. Despite some talk and notes on the subject by Dylan in his notebooks, no immediate tour supported the album. In late May 1984, a short European tour, put together by Bill Graham, featured 'Jokerman', 'License to Kill', and 'I & I'. Dylan did not tour the United States for two more years, and by that time had two newer albums to promote.

Special thanks notwithstanding, Knopfler told at least one interviewer that he was disappointed he did not get to complete the album, as he had expected after his tour. Almost as soon as Mark and Neil departed after a brief early morning session on May 5, Dylan began punching in vocals and tinkering with mixes with Abbey engineering. This went on for two months. Ian Taylor was brought in on June 5 to supervise the final mixes and he and Abbey worked to accommodate Bob's changes as seamlessly as possible. It's speculation, one informed partially by Abbey's memory, that had Knopfler returned, he would have found a changed dynamic. For example, Dylan would be in the middle of modifying one track and switch midstream to another. The more disciplined Knopfler becoming involved at that point could have at the least delayed things and at worst left the album in limbo and unreleased. Again, speculation.

In the end, the May to July efforts worked and yielded a work and sound unique in Dylan's career.

INTERRUPTION FOR AN
IMPORTANT MESSAGE

Before we resume our exploration, please: if you have never heard the songs from the *Infidels* album and sessions, stop now and buy the album, use Pandora or Spotify, or borrow a friends'. But please hear them. If you have the songs on disc, tape, computer, phone or tablet, listen again. Why? When engineer Neil Dorfsman was first contacted about this book, his response was, "I will begin by admitting that I'm a firm believer in Frank Zappa's maxim that talking about music (even the technical side of recording it) 'is like dancing about architecture.'[71]."

Ultimately, we take this as a caveat rather than a dictum. There is, however, some degree of truth in Zappa's words that demands the reader experience the music before this "dance" continues.

71 / email from Neil Dorfsman September 8, 2018

Section Two:

The Songs

The fact that Dylan saved so much of his written working materials is remarkable and what makes The Bob Dylan Archive® an unforeseen treasure chest for researchers. Why these writings were saved is something only Dylan could answer, and he has not. How they were saved is another mystery. They were not received organized. They appear to have been put in boxes at the end of whatever project was being worked on and wherever Dylan happened to be. They were not gathered together in any one particular place. At an unknown date, organizing began with the goal of offering the personal papers as part of an archive that included writings, recordings and ephemera. Somehow, thousands of pieces of paper were located and brought together. The written collection is not as substantial for the earliest years of Dylan's career but is close to overflowing thereafter.[72]

For *Infidels*, 16 songs were ultimately chosen to be recorded during the sessions.

However, those 16 do not begin to show the thought and work and dedication and effort on the part of Dylan to write and refine the songs he brought to the studio. And once in the studio, songs were recorded numerous times, with one exception, and included numerous lyric changes.

The writings included hundreds of pages of notes, verses, lyric ideas and entire songs revised time and again. The organization of this material in The archives is the result of informed "best guesses." For example, the lyrics that pertain to *Infidels* are catalogued as residing in Box 35 and Box 36. Much of it is, yet there are also *Infidels* lyrics in Box 81 and similarly related material scattered through Boxes 24, 25, 32, 82 and 98.[73] Material can be a line or two, such as just the words 'Jokerman' or 'Neighborhood Bully', and could be thoughts written down early in the composition effort, or remembered and later written as a reminder. As nearly all of the written material is undated,

---

72 / An immediate result of the "gathering" process was the discovery of many song lyrics mixed in with the *John Wesley Harding* material. It was these lyrics that led to *Lost on the River: The New Basement Tapes* produced by T-Bone Burnett

73 / Recognition and appreciation goes to author Clinton Heylin who also was at the archives for one week corresponding to one of my visits. Clinton was working on a separate project and asked if one of the songs I was researching talked about a murder. One song did, and that demonstrated the necessity of going through every box, not just the ones that were listed as relating to *Infidels*

informed guessing about the appropriateness of inclusion in discussion of an *Infidels* song have erred toward inclusion.

Within each box are folders, each intended to house the papers for a specific song. The order of the folders may or may not reflect the order of composition, but most likely do not. The same applies for the order of the papers within the folders. The papers are protected by clear plastic sheets. They are typewritten on mostly 8.5 x 11 inch white paper. At first glance, some of the typed sheets appear identical, including the same strike-outs of words. But such sheets can and do include revisions sheet by sheet. Was an early Wang or similar word processor used along with photocopying? All a researcher, using these archival materials, can do is note what is there and try to determine their place and relevance in the grand scheme of *Infidels*.

In addition to the typewritten material, much is handwritten, including the notebooks.

Included are standard papers, index cards, match books, note pads and legal paper. On some papers, the writing is in ink and pencil. On some, the handwriting seems to be in four or five different Dylan styles of script. Sometimes, the writing seems to deteriorate as the writer tires.

Many require repeated examination, including using a magnifying glass for the smallest writing, to be read successfully. I felt excitedly triumphant with each deciphering! For years, we have been provided tales of Dylan's poor eyesight, but his close vision must border on the phenomenal.

Dr. Paul Yoder (Doc)[74] was an early visitor to the archives and theorized that Dylan typed drafts of lyrics, photocopied them and then made revisions on the copies. And it seems that way, except pages of typescript seem to be identical to other drafts, but the revisions are also typewritten without any strikethroughs. So, until Dylan discusses the process, we cannot know exactly what it was.

Again, we can try and guess the order in which songs were written and rewritten. In the end, it's probably a fruitless effort. The recording sessions, indicated that Dylan did not necessarily put all his effort into the most recent version. Sometimes, he called for the "old way," and this may or may not just

---

74 / Paul Yoder is Emeritus Professor, University of Arkansas

refer to musical treatment.

We are left dealing with what we have, not what we don't. I will present a lot of information. I will offer some suppositions. But in the end, each reader may ponder his or her individual conclusions.

In terms of what we have, nearly 30 hours of complete session tapes were available for review. These are identified as master recordings and are explained as being the result of the engineer hitting the record button whenever it seemed a take was likely. As discussed in the last chapter, after months of research on the session tapes and months of back and forth, "Yes they exist, no there do not," quarter-inch two-track running studio reference tapes were located. These run tapes capture all the activities in the studio beginning late on April 16,including chit-chat, rehearsals, instructions and some control room talk-back not on the session tapes. [75] The tapes, recorded at 7.5 ips (inches per second) had never been played. In order for them to become part of the archived material, the tapes had to be properly processed and digitized. This necessitated baking the tapes at low temperature.

All tapes, including those located after the initial deposit, are now part of the archives.

The archives schedules the restoration and digitizing dependent upon the condition of the tapes, their relative importance and need for research. Budget is also a consideration. The tapes that are in greatest danger of deteriorating and being lost forever are highest priority. These newly identified *Infidels* run tapes were not in any priority before I began the research for this book.

There are nearly 55 of these tapes, and most run 66 minutes. The support of The Bob Dylan Archive® and their securing essential co-ordination and co-operation with Dylan's New York office is greatly appreciated.

The Recording Process

Bob Dylan has the reputation – self-proclaimed repeatedly – of recording live in the studio. From his first studio recording sessions in 1961, he simply

---

75 / According to an October 16, 2019 email from Assistant Engineer Josh Abbey, "I remember deciding with Neil (Dorfsman) that we should run them (quarter-inch reference tapes) at some point after the project started. Running tapes like those was not standard procedure, and I cannot remember ever doing it before or after *Infidels*. [It] Seemed like a good idea at the time!"

recorded a take of the song. Sometimes he recorded the same song many times until he and/or the producer were satisfied. On his recordings, compared to other artists of the times, there were few splices, inserts or punch-ins. In the earlier years of his career, perfection was not a goal in and of itself. Hence, in 'Memphis Blues Again', we have, "when I, he built a fire on Main Street." On 'You Angel You', "You're as, you got me."[76] Even when there was an insert, as described in the article on the recording of *Another Side of Bob Dylan*,[77] the words "romp, stomp, thankful" were delivered a little clumsily.

Infidels in some ways might be considered an experiment on Dylan's part.[78] His decision—and it was his decision—to hire a "celebrity" fellow musician as producer was one of the steps. Once Knopfler was on board, it was his responsibility to work with techniques and engineers he had become familiar with making Dire Straits albums. By hiring Knopfler, and, with him, Dorfsman, Dylan accepted contemporary methods of cutting and punching in notes and words and verses. As time went on in the project (remember, the sessions were from April 11 to May 5), Dylan seemed more comfortable with the opportunities provided by the digital recording and console. Engineer Josh Abbey: "He got used to ...(it) pretty quickly. It was the time things took that remained the biggest negative." Some of the time was Bob's choice. From May 11 until July, Dylan redid portions of his vocals and added and subtracted instrument tracks as Columbia got more anxious for things to wrap up.

A number of *Infidels* session tracks were recorded the old-fashioned way: play the song, and if needed, play it again. 'License to Kill' was a one-take song. On the other hand, 'Jokerman', 'Don't Fall Apart on Me Tonight', 'Sweetheart Like You' and 'I & I' were assembled from a lot of recordings. There is no one take of these songs that can pointed to as anything but the starting point for Dylan, Knopfler and the engineers to build upon.

---

76 / The word "scrapegoat" 'in Ballad in Plain D' is more likely an inside joke between Dylan and another person

77 / Hentoff, Nat "The Crackin', Shakin', Breakin' Sounds." The New Yorker, October 24, 1964

78 / *Empire Burlesque*, the successor album from 1985, continued the experiment. By the early Nineties, Dylan went retro, recording two solo acoustic albums. Beginning with the 2001 *Love and Theft*, Dylan used old microphones and recorded with the band around him in a circle. email from Josh Abbey, June 4, 2019

Most of the recording sessions were at night, usually beginning at 8:00 for the musicians. The engineers arrived earlier to do the set-up. After Knopfler's departure, there were some daytime sessions with Dylan.[79]

Early in my marriage, we had a jigsaw puzzle of Monet's The Water Lilies. None of the colorful individual pieces gave anything comparable to the whole. That's like 'Jokerman' and 'Sweetheart Like You' – the pieces have been assembled into a lovely whole.

The other songs, including the eight outtakes, are essentially beginning to end recordings until a preferred take was achieved. There may be instruments added or subtracted and a word here and there punched in, but the chosen track is mostly what was recorded live. In the case of 'Foot of Pride', which began as 'Too Late', over more than 50 tracks were begun, almost 20 of which were completed including several only on the run tapes. The version on The Bootleg Series Vol. 1-3 was recorded on April 29, the last day it was attempted, and shows no obvious signs of being tinkered with later.

Different tape formats and speeds were used for different purposes throughout the project.[80] For the actual live recording, 3M 32 track 1-inch digital tape captured the full band basic tracks. At any point, overdubs could be recorded on this tape. With 32 tracks available, any of the basic tracks could be "set aside." The overdub did not erase the original. At any time, rough mixes could be made using 2-track 1/4-inch analog tape running at 15 ips. At times, a rough mix might be dubbed onto a cassette for Dylan to review back at his hotel.

From the fifth day of recording, backing up the digital live recordings, 1/4-inch analog tape, running at 7.5 ips, captured everything as a run tape.

Half-inch analog tape, at 30 ips, was used for master quality sample mixes and edits. These were recorded simultaneously with U-matic[81] digital masters. The album was mastered from the edited U-matics.

---

79 / email from Josh Abbey June 4, 2019
80 / email from Josh Abbey, March 30, 2019
81 / U-matic tape was developed by SONY for digital material and was the medium of choice for years in commercial television and advertising production. The tape is contained in a plastic housing that unloads onto the recording/playback equipment

Safety copies were made of the 32-track digital multi-track recordings. These were backups and were not used in production. The session tapes in the archives are mp3 copies of stereo rough mixes made at an Iron Mountain facility[82] in Hollywood, California, in September 2016. They were made from the 32-track 45 ips tapes. They can be different mixes from the album, or from anything else put together by Knopfler, Dylan or the engineers.

The written documentation about the sessions, when not included in the stored tape boxes, was reconstructed from archival information gathered by Michael Krogsgaard in 1996 and from data compiled for Special Rider Music in 2012.

Organization

Each song forms a chapter. While different printed sources form the discussion, such as those on *Bobdylan.com*, 2014's *The Lyrics* from Simon and Schuster. Your ears may tell you different but the official approved lyrics allowed for reproduction are from Bob Dylan *The Lyrics 1961-2012*, also from Simon and Schuster in 2016. In describing the development of a song, fair use allows quoting of several words of a draft in sequence and also paraphrasing. The changes as a song progresses can be followed with these limitations. The same parameters apply when I discuss the session takes of each song. The reader will get the idea. To help make comparison easier, each line of the official lyrics for each song are numbered.

The order of the chapters, since we do not have dates for the order that work began with writing the songs, will be in order of when the songs were first attempted in the recording sessions. Thus, we begin with 'Blind Willie McTell'. Within each chapter, written versions are discussed, followed by the recorded versions. The first 15 of these chapters (Chapters 4-19) cover the songs Dylan wrote and published, followed by unpublished songs from the sessions, including covers. Next are written songs, which are more or less complete but not recorded and finally, the parts of songs and

82 / Iron Mountain is a data storage and management firm with facilities throughout the United States. Much if not all of Columbia Records tape archives are stored at Iron Mountain facilities. The Hollywood Digital Studio Iron Mountain used has one of the few surviving 3M digital recording machines

instrumentals that complete sessions. An appendix lists what was done on each day of the sessions.

Extensive footnotes amplify the narrative, and will be found within each chapter. For the convenience of everyone, the citation BDA refers to The Bob Dylan Archive®.

SECTION TWO INTRO

4:

Blind Willie McTell

Published Lyrics
Blind Willie McTell

1	Seen the arrow on the doorpost
2	Saying, "This land is condemned
3	All the way from New Orleans To Jerusalem"
4	I traveled through East Texas
5	Where many martyrs fell
6	And I can tell you one thing, nobody can sing the blues
7	Like Blind Willie McTell
8	Well, I heard that hoot owl singing
9	As they were taking down the tents
10	The stars above the barren trees
11	Were his only audience
12	Them charcoal gypsy maidens
13	Can strut their feathers well
14	And I can tell you one thing nobody can sing the blues
15	Like Blind Willie McTell
16	See them big plantations burning
17	Hear the cracking of the whips
18	Smell that sweet magnolia blooming
19	See the ghosts of slavery ships
20	I can hear them tribes a-moaning
21	Hear that undertaker's bell
22	Nobody can sing the blues
23	Like Blind Willie McTell[83]

83 / The latest approved Lyrics book, *Bob Dylan, Bob Dylan The Lyrics 1961-2012* (New York, Simon & Schuster), 2016. It differs from *The Lyrics*. published in 2014, also by Simon & Schuster. For 2016 edition, the highlighted recorded and previously published verse was omitted and the 'I can tell you one thing' words, first recorded by The Band in 2003 and used by Dylan in concert, are inserted

24 There's a woman by the river

25 With some fine young handsome man

26 He's dressed up like a squire

27 Bootlegged whiskey in his hand

28 Some of them died in battle

29 Some of them survived as well

30 And I can tell you one thing nobody can sing the blues

30 Like Blind Willie McTell

32 Well, God is in His heaven

33 And we all want what's his

34 But power and greed and corruptible seed

35 Seem to be all that there is

36 I'm gazing out the window

37 Of the St. James Hotel

38 And I can tell you one thing nobody can sing the blues

39 Like Blind Willie McTell[84]

Writing

'Blind Willie McTell'[85] has the distinction of being the first song recorded for Infidels. (That is, if one does not count a few lines of verse and chorus for 'Jokerman' during the initial warm ups when the record button was pressed on April 11.) It also is considered by more than a few, including those who compile such lists, as being one of Dylan's finest songs. And it is also used as Exhibit One of the curious/perverse choices he made during his career regarding what does or does not get released.

84 / The lyrics reprinted are based on *bobdylan.com*. A previous source for lyrics is the 2014 publication *The Lyrics*. The book differs from the online version in style, as the song is presented in five four-line verses. The book differs from bob dylan.com Line 20 and has the tribes "moaning," not "a-moaning." Line 11 "were" becomes "was" in the book. In line 27 of bd.com, the handsome man holds "bootlegged whiskey," while the book says it's "bootleg."

85 / McTell, born William Samuel McTier, recorded under many different names from 1927 until his death in 1956. His blues style was more country than Delta. Dylan recorded McTell's 'Broke Down Engine' for 1992s *Good As I Been To You* and took the title 'Lonesome Day Blues' for a dissimilar song on 2001s *Love And Theft*

While 'Blind Willie McTell' was the first song recorded during the *Infidels* sessions on April 11, and the last on May 5, it was not released until February 1991[86]. His first concert performance of the song did not come until August 5, 1997, in Montreal. "I started playing it live because I heard the Band doing it. Most likely it was a demo, probably showing the musicians how it should go. It was never developed fully, I never got around to completing it. There wouldn't have been any other reason for leaving it off the record. It's like taking a painting by Monet or Picasso – goin' to his house and lookin' at a half-finished painting and grabbing it and selling it to people who are 'Picasso fans.' It was Dylan's decision as an artist whether to release the song or not, or whether he considered it finished or not recorded correctly. But it certainly was not a demo, as its history of eleven attempts of recording the song demonstrates.

'Blind Willie McTell' is heavy with mood, memory, the spirit of days past, the doomed "Southern way of life" pre-Civil War. A dead way of life: barren trees, burning plantations, phantom ships with their human cargo. Perhaps some of those ships sailed into the mist of another song from this era. Importantly, these descriptions lead to a present-day observation on the nature of man, "power and greed and corruptible seed." Perhaps the reflections of the destruction earlier in the song are the product of this flaw in the species.

The written lyrics have such a small evidentiary trail, it argues for the song being almost fully formed from the start. The archives presents briefer written history than for most of the other songs which were recorded at The Power Station.[87]

Only one written version of 'Blind Willie McTell' exists and it is the same one reproduced for a brief time on the website for Heaven's Door whiskey. It has five typewritten verses[88] and one-handwritten sixth verse. At the top of the page are what appear to be typed thoughts for lines before the verses for the song appear. The "gypsy maidens" of Line 12 were once the "face of an angel, remembered "well." The gypsy maidens then reminded the singer of when he first heard Mr McTell. Dylan was still deciding if the undertaker in Line 21 should be a coroner ringing a bell.

---

86 / *The Bootleg Series: Rare and Unreleased Vol. 1-3*

87 / There are no written lyrics for Sweetheart Like You in the archives other than those prepared for copyright purposes after recording

88 / Archives 2016.01 B35 F11 01

In the first verse, Line 2, condemned land was initially "property."[89]

In line 8 hoot owl was written in to replace "I sang a song at sundown", as he uses a fence to rest his foot.

From that point, the song deviates only in minor fashion from the known finished lyrics, with, however, the handwritten extra verse, which has the narrator and Betty Grable "trying to stay warm" in Nashville[90]. The rhyme for McTell is "I've known some Creole belle."

Only one other written hint of the song is in materials in Tulsa. It could be the germ of an idea, it could be a reminder for what Dylan intended work on. It could be sudden thought of a lyric change. At the bottom of an early version of 'Jokerman' Dylan wrote, "I hear the tribes A moaning...Nobody sings the blues Like BWM."[91]

And that is all there is of the writing.

All kinds of assorted folks have had a go at the meaning of the song. One can read the "gypsy maidens" as slaves or working girls. Perhaps they were in New Orleans marching in a funeral.

Some, like Michael Gray in his *Bob Dylan Encyclopedia* makes his case for the song being about death.

As indicated above, the spirit of the song as constructed by the setting of the location and time, and the choice of words, is an evocation of mood. A change in the flow and a break in the mood comes with the sharpness of the word "God," a hard sound in the second word in the final verse. The previous verses all start with soft sounds. The switch takes the song to the present day "gazing out the window." The writer observes the current nature of "all that there is," grabs the listener and reminds him or her that perhaps all one can do is sing the blues. None of us can do it as well as our predecessors. Is it a celebration of McTell or despair at our shortcomings?

Recording

'Blind Willie McTell' is a song of a ghostly past remembered as if in a dream.

---

89 / *This Property Is Condemned* was originally a one-act play by Tennessee Williams and was rewritten and produced as a film in 1966

90 / Nashville is where the non-bootleg Heaven's Door Whisky would be headquartered 35 years later. "Grable" rhymes with "Gable" which is in the next recorded song

91 / Archives

It is supported by an atmospheric organ and driven by Dylan's piano, inspired vocal and harmonica. The melody is clearly 'St. James Infirmary Blues', and the lyrics could have been composed specifically for that structure. The presence of a "St. James hotel" in the final verse encourages the listener to consider the new song as being a continuation of the former. 'St. James Infirmary Blues' had many antecedents and the origins of that song are murky to the point of being unknowable. Some see an extremely loose structural and chord progression as a relationship in Dylan's song to McTell's Dyin Crapshooter Blues'.[92]. It's a tenuous assertion.

For the first studio date, Dylan and the album band likely got past initial greetings and down to loosening up on their instruments before any recording began. Once the digital tape started rolling, about twenty-two minutes of playing, including some seconds of Dave Dudley's 1963 hit 'Six Days On the Road', helped engineers find the right mic arrangements, recording levels and balance in the headphones. The band ran through typical jams, a few minutes of rough backing of 'Jokerman', with Dylan singing a few scattered words and, probably, playing a guitar that is way down in the mix. He tests some harp playing, and then moves to the piano, where some instrumental "Blind Willie McTell" is played.

At 24 minutes and 20 seconds, the recording sheet notes, "vocal begins," and recording is now underway. Dylan sings the first verse, followed by a guitar break and two sections of harmonica playing as Knopfler and Taylor intertwine guitar parts. Dylan then sings the "hoot owl" verse, and then playing halts. The song had been taken at an up-tempo pace. After Dylan asks Clark about a synthesizer, the song restarts at a more determined stately tempo. The stop at this point might have been to accommodate a tape change. As has been noted, the 3M digital tape, allows for 32 tracks and also had a length of 32 minutes.

When they pick up again, Dylan leads with a high-pitched hum of the melody (falsetto if actually sung) and then sings the second verse as Taylor plays some

<hr>

92 / The lengths to which music lovers will go to know all there is about a song is demonstrated by the excellent 'I Went Down St. James Infirmary'" by Robert W. Harrow. Harrow investigates links, debunks theories and compares and contrasts similar lyrics and melodies from the 1300s to the age of recorded music. He makes a very good case that 'Dyin' Crapshooter Blues' was not composed by McTell. So it is quite possible Dylan borrows from someone who borrows. This is an irony probably not lost on Dylan, whose knowledge of song exceeds mine and possibly any reader

signature slide. The next take introduces what would be the opening for the song for several days. Clark plays some church-like organ licks, the drums kick in, after which Dylan immediately begins singing. While not a perfect take, the song is there immediately, its specialness evident.

Dylan takes his band on a brief detour into a make-it-up-as-we-go riff called 'Oh Babe' with dummy lyrics. (See Chapter 22).

'Blind Willie' is back with a two-minute slow attempt marred by Dylan reaching too high vocally on "the stars above the barren trees." The attempt stops after the second verse, and Dylan says "Something about that seems..."

The next take dispenses with the organ introduction and is the "full-band" version of the song that many people prefer to the released piano and acoustic guitar version. Dylan and the musicians absolutely nail it! The sheet accompanying the reel notes "Good," which someone amended to "Best?" One reason the organ intro is not included in this take is that Dylan began playing and singing while Clark was using the rest room, returning for the third verse.[93] In the second line, Dylan has a percussive burst of a stifled laugh. After Josh Abbey discussed with Dylan a month or so later the technology of punch-ins, this flaw could have been easily corrected. But once the sessions ended, Dylan did not seem to have interest in the song.

'Blind Willie McTell' was left until a week later, when Dylan would again attempt to capture the song at the end of a day otherwise dedicated to 'Sweetheart Like You'.

On April 18, when the team returns to the song, some opening glitches occur when Dylan can't hear his piano or vocals in his earphones. This is quickly overcome, and after some quick warmup notes, the group goes into a take with a reggae tempo somewhat like that used for 'Man Gave Names to All the Animals' during the 1981 tour and Springsteen on 'Part Man Part Monkey'. It's bouncy and conflicts with the previous mood of the song. Dylan's vocal is perfunctory. Nevertheless, the engineers marked it "good" on their sheets. A second reggae track is recorded ("great"). I beg to differ: it's better when compared to the preceding but still does not fit the song and Dylan is straining at the top of his register to try and impart some seriousness to the vocal. It is a

93 / Interview with Alan Clark

wonderful showcase for Robbie Shakespeare's bass playing and Sly Dunbar's emphatic drumming. Despite this, or perhaps because of it, an atmospheric song demanding nuance is recorded with none of it. An extended instrumental runout takes the track to over seven-and-one-half minutes. Bob plays a bit of the song on the piano, and the day's recording ends.

May 5 is the last day of scheduled recording sessions for *Infidels*. Only 'Blind Willie McTell' is worked on and laid down. Knopfler joins Dylan's piano with an acoustic guitar for one last try at recording the masterpiece that has been evading them. After less than a minute of warm up, Dylan says "We'll give it one pass."

"Yeh yeh," Mark replies. "We don't have to use it, it's up to you." It may be the producer has argued for this last attempt. At the end of the take, Dylan asks, "What do you think?" The answer leads to one final take, at slower pace, and a very poignant vocal. It is the first of the two takes that is selected for a tape of the songs under consideration, along with the full-band version from April 11.

And that would seem to be that. The band version of the song was almost instantaneously bootlegged, possibly from a cassette one of the musicians had with him in Europe that summer. A few months later the acoustic version was bootlegged from a tape submitted to the Library of Congress for Copyright purposes. Thus began the incredulity around the suppression of 'Blind Willie' until release in 1991. There is a short coda to the story of the recording. In the mixing or overdub efforts, one or two electric guitars were dubbed onto the first acoustic version. It is interesting to listen to, but horrible to hear!

5:

Don't Fall Apart on Me Tonight

Published Lyrics
Don't Fall Apart on me Tonight

1	Just a minute before you leave, girl
2	Just a minute before you touch the door
3	What is it that you're trying to achieve, girl?
4	Do you think we can talk about it some more?
5	You know, the streets are filled with vipers
6	Who've lost all ray of hope
7	You know, it ain't even safe no more
8	In the palace of the Pope
9	Don't fall apart on me tonight
10	I just don't think that I could handle it
11	Don't fall apart on me tonight
12	Yesterday's just a memory
13	Tomorrow is never what it's supposed to be
14	And I need you, yeah
15	Come over here from over there, girl
16	Sit down here. You can have my chair
17	I can't see us goin' anywhere, girl
18	The only place open is a thousand miles away and I can't take you there
19	I wish I'd have been a doctor
20	Maybe I'd have saved some life that had been lost
21	Maybe I'd have done some good in the world
22	'Stead of burning every bridge I crossed
23	Don't fall apart on me tonight
24	I just don't think that I could handle it
25	Don't fall apart on me tonight
26	Yesterday's just a memory
27	Tomorrow is never what it's supposed to be
28	And I need you, oh, yeah
29	I ain't too good at conversation, girl
30	So you might not know exactly how I feel

31   But if I could, I'd bring you to the mountaintop, girl
32   And build you a house made out of stainless steel
33   But it's like I'm stuck inside a painting
34   That's hanging in the Louvre
35   My throat start to tickle and my nose itches
36   But I know that I can't move
37   Don't fall apart on me tonight
38   I just don't think that I could handle it
39   Don't fall apart on me tonight
40   Yesterday's gone but the past lives on
41   Tomorrow's just one step beyond
42   And I need you, oh, yeah

43   Who are these people who are walking towards you?
44   Do you know them or will there be a fight?
45   With their humorless smiles so easy to see through
46   Can they tell you what's wrong from what's right?
47   Do you remember St. James Street
48   Where you blew Jackie P.'s mind?
49   You were so fine, Clark Gable would have fell at your feet
50   And laid his life on the line

51   Let's try to get beneath the surface waste, girl
52   No more booby traps and bombs
53   No more decadence and charm
54   No more affection that's misplaced, girl
55   No more mudcake creatures lying in your arms
56   What about that millionaire with the drumsticks in his pants?
57   He looked so baffled and so bewildered
58   When he played and we didn't dance
59   Don't fall apart on me tonight
60   I just don't think that I could handle it
61   Don't fall apart on me tonight
62   Yesterday's just a memory

63   Tomorrow is never what it's supposed to be
64   And I need you, yeah

Writing

The first page of the January 1983 notebook shows some of the thought process leading to the development of 'Don't Fall Apart on Me Tonight'. Words about hidden feelings and preventing these feelings from being known may be a direct precursor to Line 32 of the published lyrics. Also, the note "yesterday's dead" may be an earlier version of "yesterday's just a memory" or "yesterday's gone."[94]

One thought constant through many drafts of the song appears on page six of the first notebook. Dylan wrote, "wished I'd been a doctor, maybe I'd a saved a few lives that have been lost." The recorded verse is nearly identical, and the notebook writing goes on about regret for "burning every bridge I crossed."(Line 24.) As noted earlier, words written in a notebook do not establish them as the first time the thought came to Dylan, but the words do show importance enough for him to write the thought down and remember it, even while aboard his boat.

On the eleventh notebook page, the word "Viper" appears and 17 pages later, in the midst of lyrics ultimately destined for "I & I," the lyrics for Lines 6 and 7 appear. No other traces of 'Don't Fall Apart on Me Tonight' appear in the notebook.

The Archives has nine drafts of lyrics for 'Don't Fall Apart on Me Tonight'. The elements that remain the same throughout include regrets for not having been a doctor, although sometime an alternate career as a waiter or clerk instead of a bridge burner; an inability to communicate through conversation; an attempt to coax the girl who is on the verge of leaving to instead cross a room and come to him; a feeling of being trapped in a painting—an image for others to view while he must stay immobile; rejection of decadence and charm; a street scene featuring a Clark Gable name-check; and "bewildered" people of different levels of power and status with drumsticks in their pants.

It is nearly impossible to pinpoint the first written version of the song. The lyrics folder includes a three-by-five-inch paper and pencil draft with a number of the key phrases: "humorless smiles," "Clark Gable would've fallen at your feet" and "walking towards you."

94 / Archives 2016.01 B99 F01

The chorus (lines 11-16 and thereafter) does not appear on every written version.

Regret the narrator expresses at not having been a doctor (line 21) evolves from the one version's thought that it might have been something he would have liked. However, he writes he was only trained, or suited, to be a waiter or a clerk. The verse ultimately reflects an awareness of rebelliousness and diffidence (line 24).

If there is a narrative thread it is simply that the writer wants a girl to stay with him. He wants to try, difficult as it may be, to explain something about himself to her so that she might understand him and how much he'd like to do for her. A group of other people intrude.

Are they acquaintances of hers? He reminds her of Napoleon Street where she stunned Clark Gable (line 51). The writer pleads that they move beyond surfaces and misplaced affections and practically demands her to abandon those who might misuse her (line 57).[95] Finally, she's asked about "that millionaire" or hypocrite, or midnight rambler. Whoever, he wore, depending on the draft, long white robes and had menus or drumsticks in his pants. None of them could understand why the narrator would not dance to their tune.

The song is pleading with the girl not to fall apart. Yet, it is the narrator who seems at a breaking point—obsessing about old memories, repeating, "I don't know if I can handle it." This is an ambiguity typical of so many Dylan songs.

A coherent song remarkably came out of the chaos of these drafts. The work was purposeful, and Dylan evidently intended it as a key song on the album he was progressing toward.[96] It was the second song attempted in the recording sessions and was attempted 15 times

It was chosen to close *Infidels*, but, it was never performed in concert.

Recording

Laying down the tracks for 'Don't Fall Apart on Me Tonight' started with

95 / One of the seemingly inexplicable phrases is "mud cake creatures." It could refer to a driller, a baker or a sexual practice. Or it could just be three words put together. Your guess is as good as any
96 / One draft, except for one verse, has a narrative that is more consistent with what became 'Foot of Pride'
97 / It may actually have been a session conducted completely on April 12. These recordings begin on a reel separate from 'Blind Willie McTell'. The first tape box says April 11, but all the written sheets say April 12. The second tape box for 'Don't Fall Apart' is April 12. The sheet inside that box titles the song 'Don't Fall Apart On Me Like That'

rehearsals toward the end of April 11[97]. Dylan had settled on lyrics, chord changes and melody(although no final written form before a later copyright version is in the archives.). After several false starts (in one Dylan complains his guitar sounds like "a rubber band,") he and his band began working in earnest on 'Don't Fall Apart on Me Tonight'.

Initially, the song is taken at a very slow, almost majestic pace, with Clark's piano and Knopfler's guitar taking a dominant role in a nearly 12-minute recording. Dylan's voice is gentle but not beseeching. The vocal is more deliberate than later, when he gained comfort with the melody. He has not yet found the words that become Line 18 and is asking the girl to "set your wild spirit down and hush." The musicians play out for an extra five minutes after the vocal ends.

This take is followed by some experimenting with a reggae treatment for a short period, until Dylan says, "Nah." A brief instrumental lead-in sounds somewhat like Bob Marley's 'No Woman No Cry'. Dylan requests, "Let's do it all the way through, then listen to it, see what sounds right, what sounds wrong and then do it again. I want to play it so they can dance to it in an old folks' home."

With Clark on organ and Dylan on piano, the band executes this instruction scrupulously, and Dylan gives a more comfortable and slightly more nuanced vocal. The bridge does not yet smoothly fit into the song, which Dylan observes with a "well." On Napoleon Street they "watched old Jackie P dine." As the song concludes, Dylan says, "We've gotta burn that one," and one can guess he doesn't mean to burn it to disc.

A couple of reggae style verses are tried, and then comes the reel unequivocally identified as April 12.[98] The argument for it actually being a separate day can be made by the lyrics in Line 18 being the final ones and the feel of the song is very close to the released version. It can also indicate a lunch-break lyric refining with all takes on the same day. The reggae spirit is preserved but not dominant. The engineer, who had called the previous take "good," notes this as "hot".

The crew moved from the key of C to A as Dylan worked to find the right feel and pitch for his vocal. The takes still show that the bridge needs work to blend in musically, and on Napoleon Street the girl is asked to remember "where I put

98. / On the sheet marked April 12, the engineer identifies the song as 'Don't Fall Apart On Me Like That'

my life on the line." As the song finishes, Dylan expresses his dissatisfaction. They then try a faster pace and a very "Dylan styled speak-sing vocal," but it breaks down at the bridge and Dylan again expresses frustration.

After the band takes a break, they try another complete take in C. After a reel change, Dylan wants to try it in E, requiring a higher vocal pitch. The rough mix that was made for the archival digitization project is, in fact, rough with all the instruments placed closely together.

An engineer noted the take as being "no good." Properly mixed, however, it seems it could have been considered for the final vocal take if the instruments were re-recorded.

Finally, back to the key of C, they find the master take. The engineer noted a "good vocal...middle 8." It's also noted as including overdubs, which is probably why the this is the only take that substitutes St. James Street for Napoleon Street and credits the narrator's companions as blowing Jackie T's mind.

Michael Krogsgaard, a Scandinavian researcher, had the approval of Dylan's office and put together a session history in the early Nineties. He attributed the released take of the song to the first take on reel 4 of the recordings. From all that can now be heard and reviewed from the archival documentation, the evidence favors the final recording of the song as being the one chosen to overdub and release.

Nine lyric drafts, eight complete takes and numerous incomplete takes and false starts and the eventual album closer is completed. Whether 'Don't Fall Apart on Me Tonight' is as strong as other songs on the album, or songs left off, is a whole other subject for debate. The song was important to Dylan.

CHAPTER 5 / DON'T FALL APART ON ME TONIGHT

6:

Jokerman

Published Lyrics
Jokerman

1	Standing on the waters casting your bread
2	While the eyes of the idol with the iron head are glowing
3	Distant ships sailing into the mist
4	You were born with a snake in both of your fists while a hurricane was blowing
5	Freedom just around the corner for you
6	But with the truth so far off, what good will it do?
7	Jokerman dance to the nightingale tune
8	Bird fly high by the light of the moon
9	Oh, oh, oh, Jokerman
10	So swiftly the sun sets in the sky
11	You rise up and say goodbye to no one
12	Fools rush in where angels fear to tread
13	Both of their futures, so full of dread, you don't show one
14	Shedding off one more layer of skin
15	Keeping one step ahead of the persecutor within
16	Jokerman dance to the nightingale tune
17	Bird fly high by the light of the moon
18	Oh, oh, oh, Jokerman
19	You're a man of the mountains, you can walk on the clouds
20	Manipulator of crowds, you're a dream twister
21	You're going to Sodom and Gomorrah
22	But what do you care? Ain't nobody there would want to marry your sister
23	Friend to the martyr, a friend to the woman of shame
24	You look into the fiery furnace, see the rich man without any name
25	Jokerman dance to the nightingale tune
26	Bird fly high by the light of the moon
27	Oh, oh, oh, Jokerman

28   Well, the Book of Leviticus and Deuteronomy
29   The law of the jungle and the sea are your only teachers
30   In the smoke of the twilight on a milk-white steed
31   Michelangelo indeed could've carved out your features
32   Resting in the fields, far from the turbulent space
33   Half asleep near the stars with a small dog licking your face
34   Jokerman dance to the nightingale tune
35   Bird fly high by the light of the moon
36   Oh, oh, oh, Jokerman

37   Well, the rifleman's stalking the sick and the lame
38   Preacherman seeks the same, who'll get there first is uncertain
39   Nightsticks and water cannons, tear gas, padlocks
40   Molotov cocktails and rocks behind every curtain
41   False-hearted judges dying in the webs that they spin
42   Only a matter of time 'til night comes steppin' in
43   Jokerman dance to the nightingale tune
44   Bird fly high by the light of the moon
45   Oh, oh, oh, Jokerman

46   It's a shadowy world, skies are slippery grey
47   A woman just gave birth to a prince today and dressed him in scarlet
48   He'll put the priest in his pocket, put the blade to the heat
49   Take the motherless children off the street
50   And place them at the feet of a harlot
51   Oh, Jokerman, you know what he wants
52   Oh, Jokerman, you don't show any response
53   Jokerman dance to the nightingale tune
54   Bird fly high by the light of the moon
55   Oh, oh, oh, Jokerman

Writing

'Jokerman' is a true album opener. It kicks you in the face, lifts you up, boxes your ears and generally announces "this is something different." Dylan has said it's one of the "island songs:" "'Jokerman' kinda came to me in the islands. It's very mystical. The shapes there, and shadows, seem to be so ancient. The song was sorta inspired by these spirits they call jumbis."[99]

'Jokerman' is a lyrically dense song, developed over at least 13 drafts before recording, several changes during the April sessions and another revision in either May or June 1983. It's hard to get even a feel for when the idea for the song was born. The word "Nightengale"(sic) is found boxed on the third page of the first notebooks previously mentioned.[100] (In fact, the word is in earlier writings including a discarded line in early versions of 'Visions of Johanna'.) The word "nightingale" also shows up in one of the early drafts of 'Foot of Pride' or 'Too Late', as it was initially titled. Professor Nightengale is one of many characters populating the song as it evolves in many, many drafts. The words "clipper ship" are on the same page as the "boxed" nightingale, and early recorded versions mention the "Yankee Clipper." One sheet consists of only of lines of two words each: "snooper[man], iron head, tear gas."[101] Finally, there is a stray reference to "the sailor and the jokerman."[102]

Some of the images seem tied to earlier works. Could the "distant ships" in line 3 be the same ones that are "distant ships of liberty" in the *Shot of Love* outtake 'Caribbean Wind'? While they brought liberty in the earlier song, in 'Jokerman', "freedom is just around the corner." The imagery is similar to the ghostly slavery ships from 'Blind Willie McTell'. When ships come in, they may not necessarily bring good news.

The song practically sits up and begs to be taken as autobiographical. Except, Dylan does not write openly autobiographical songs, at least not since 1964's 'Ballad in Plain D'.[103] "What he may do is toy with the Dylan myth, using the "I is another" point of view. Certainly, the mythical Dylan character "sheds off....

99 / Loder, Kurt, *Bob Dylan: Recovering Christian*, (*Rolling Stone*, San Francisco) June 21, 1984. A jumbo, or jumble, is a ghost or a malevolent spirit. The word may have the same origin as zombie 100 / BDA 2016.07.B99 F0

101 / BDA Archives 2016.01.B32.F03.06

102 / BDA Archives 2016.01.B82.F09.01

103 / "'Ballad In Plain D', starkly and regretfully, recounted the end of Dylan's romantic relationship with Suze Rotolo. Interviewed by Bill Flanagan in 1985 for his book *Written in My Soul* Dylan said " [on] that one I look back and I say, ' must have been a real schmuck to write that.' I look back at that particular one and say, of all the songs I've written, maybe I could have left that alone."

skin (personae),[104] manipulates crowds, twists dreams and is a heroic figure to many—"Michelangelo indeed could have carved out your features." In 1983, the current incarnation of the Dylan myth included his perceived spiritual journey, referenced by lines 28 and 29.

But wait—the Jokerman could be Christ standing on the water, casting bread. Who else was a better friend to the martyrs or shamed women? Or is it the Antichrist? The newly born prince dressed in scarlet certainly seems threatening, especially when "you know what he wants."[105]

Finally, the impassive mythic-Dylan, addressed as the Jokerman, doesn't "show any response." This wording is included on a page of disjointed verse that is otherwise unrelated to any of the 'Jokerman' lyrics: "You know what he wants, you don't show any response/emotion."[106]

As noted earlier, it is impossible to precisely pinpoint when any of the lyrics were written. We can make an educated guess about what thoughts precede the heavy work of writing a song. Dylan is a good harvester of usable words and thoughts previously written down and, unlike Van Morrison, say, doesn't repeat specific lines throughout his body of work.

What could be the first draft attempt at 'Jokerman' comes as a fourth verse in the middle of a draft of 'Man of Peace'. Instead of "standin' on the water," it opens "standing on the corner with your hat in your hand." Freedom is around the corner, "independence, truth and liberty too." It seems as if this part of 'Jokerman', which could have been a separate work in progress, intruded into Dylan's thoughts when he was working on 'Man of Peace'. It is not a verse for that song, as the meter and rhyming scheme do not fit.[107]

The first workings of the opening line have trial words such as "standing in

---

104 / The video for 'Jokerman', created by George Lois and Larry 'Ratso' Sloman, was permitted by Dylan to present a rapid succession of photos of the singer changing his image over years

105 / In Archives Box 36, Folder 9, 18 sheets may or may not associate chronologically with the Infidels period. One clue that they might is a reference to "Angel Flying Too Close to the Ground." A couplet winds up in "Death Is Not the End." And four lines looking to the sky, a melting heart, no desire to sleep and "You know what he wants, you don't show any response/emotion." Mostly, the papers seem to be abandoned verses, random thoughts about playing a role, questions about the true self and being a stranger in his own home.

106 / Ibid F09.15

107 / BDA Box 35.F03.02

the river catching fish with your hands." The iron-headed idol with glowing eyes is a man with a golden arm in early versions. The concept of freedom around the corner and far-off truth are constants, as is the image of shedding skins and evading the "persecutor within."

Over the course of writing, Dylan works with various animal imagery. The wolf, in particular, is given a number of tries: "a friend to the wolf," "the secrets of the wolf,"[108] "holding a wolf." Most ominous, the woman in line 47 gives birth not to a prince, but a wolf[109] following a labor that extends to 12 months.

In several versions, the 'Jokerman' has the voice of a parrot in his heart, a parrot that sometimes speaks in German. In several versions, he is guided by a peacock through "perilous straights." The cumulative impact of the various beasts that for a time populate the lyrics is to make the Jokerman a close relative to the subject of the song in which that one verse a few paragraphs back first appears – 'Man of Peace'. Along the way, there is a notation directly tying in to Revelations. Indeed, he writes that the New Testament "tells you that the tigers of the sea have been your only teacher." These words would impart a much different interpretation from the teachers of the finished song being "Leviticus and Deuteronomy."

The Jokerman is depicted as working through many roles. His life is described as a series of breaths, an individual who suffers "like a madman." Before a drunk, presumably the Jokerman, winds up in the street, he's been reciting Keats and Shelley and ancient prayers.

Ultimately, the existence that is depicted throughout drafting the lyrics leads to the final two verses. The image of stalking rifleman or preacher man evolves from the Jokerman himself being an animal preacher, a preacher of darkness. Whoever it is consistently wields nightsticks, water cannons and the like.

The shadowy world described beginning in line 36 was envisioned for the song's conclusion early in the writing. At one time, what the birth meant for the world was significantly more ominous. The wolf would "divide your house" and turn you against your neighbor. The prince will do worse: he'll "take your soul" and "take your children as his sacrifice." This is certainly a bleaker fate than taking "motherless children off the street."

Lines 23 and 24 at one time portrayed someone closely examining the world,

108 / "...the moon and the elf." The Jokerman knows all secrets but for any about himself
109 / all ibid

being a "king among nations...a stranger at home." In Notebook 1, there are thoughts which became part of 'I & I'(Chapter 12). On an untrodden path the narrator muses about whispering to a deaf mute "who made me feel like a stranger in my own home."[110]

The folio of 'Jokerman' lyrics held in the archives indicate that Dylan was still working, writing new lyrics and making choices from what he'd produced previously, even as he began recording the song. There is either a race between a preacher man and a rifleman, the outcome of which is uncertain, only the preacher man telling of a predetermined "world to come." There is a sermon that all the weaponry—tear gas, Molotov cocktails—cannot drown out. The woman who gives birth either does so on the "Yankee Clipper" or is dressed in scarlet or under a blanket of scarlet. In some drafts, she may be Joan of Arc and is turned into a stripper or a harlot. The priests at this point are not in a pocket, but are turned "into pimps that make old men bark."

The purpose of sharing these choices (and the many more not covered here), is not to illustrate how strange Dylan can be in coming up with lyrics. Rather, it is to lay out what hard work and continued effort he requires of himself. It appears he lets his imagination loose and does not narrow his choices as much as collect them all before synthesizing a narrative that becomes the song.

'Jokerman' is a strong work. But it could well be that so much hard work causes a writer to lose his own connection to his work. Dylan spoke with writer Paul Zollo about 'Jokerman' and 'Infidels' in 1991: "That's a song that got away from me. Lots of songs on that album got away from me. They just did... They hung around too long. They were better before they were tampered with. Of course, it was me tampering with them. Yeah, that could have been a good song. It could have been."[111]

Well, it certainly is a very, very good song.

One person who agreed that it is was Andrew K. Smith, a British designer who created a typeface which he named 'Jokerman', after the song.

Recording

The 'Jokerman' we hear on the album is like one of the rare earth elements

110 / BDA 2016.01.B99 F01.27
111 / Zollo 78.

atomic scientists created by bombarding uranium with neutrons and creating something that did not exist previously. The released version never was played or sung in the way we've heard it since 1983. It is a miracle of digital technology and perseverance. What began in the early spring was completed in summer. The first run-through of 'Jokerman' starts the session on April 13. It's a five-minute instrumental take. After that is an apparently spontaneous Fifties-style slow rocker called 'Try Baby', that runs for eight minutes. Then, it seems like an attempt at 'Jokerman' was stopped and recorded over by a blues workout. After three more time-wasters ('Columbus Stockade Blues',[112] 'A Couple More Years'[113] and 'Do Re Mi',[114]) they return to 'Jokerman'. Dylan sings the first line and remarks, "It seems too familiar," and suggests they drop a transition chord in the second bar. Dylan's piano drives the band ahead.

At this time, lines 12 and 13 are "No store bought shirt for you on your back, one of the women must sit in the shack and sew one." It's strange that these lines were chosen for recording. The final (and published) verse appears in many of the drafts with seemingly earlier versions of other verses. The lines about fools rushing in is from Alexander Pope, and has been used in a popular song as a title[115] and as a line in a song Dylan covered, 'I Can't Help Falling in Love with You'.

The attempt at 'Jokerman' stops after two-and-a-half minutes and is followed by nearly eight minutes of blues. Now, the first complete take of 'Jokerman' takes place. Shakespeare's bass supplies a strong foundation, Clark's organ flies with the nightingale. Line 37 has the preacher man "talking' with a big bass drum" about the predetermined "world to come." The three complete takes from April 13 feature the Joan of Arc to stripper scenario, as well as,"priests into pimps." No harmonica plays on this first complete take.

The next take, at over seven minutes, is, at least, part of the musical bed underneath the version overdubbed with a new vocal for the original "keeper" until it was edited and overdubbed with new vocals, harmonica and guitar in June. In Krogsgaard's session list, he does not indicate which take is the one on the record. It may well be a composite of this and the following take. A brief

---

112 / Attributed to Doc Watson
113 / Written by Shel Silverstein
114 / Written by Woody Guthrie
115 / 'Fools Rush In(Where Angels Fear To Tread) ' by Johnny Mercer and Rube Bloom

harmonica solo plays at the end of this take. The engineer has marked the take "good groove @ end".

The final April 13 recording of 'Jokerman', "great," according to the engineer's notes.

This take includes no harmonica break or end solo.

Krogsgaard found information years ago that indicating that 'Jokerman', on the *Infidels* album, was a composite resulting from final work on the track on July 20. Sheets indicate up to 16 takes, which may have been how they were documenting the different vocal overdubs. For our purposes, we know how the song sounded as Dylan began recording, in different April session versions, in some of the overdubs and edits in May and June and the released version finalized in July. We may never have the 100 per cent complete story of how the track came together. However, it is fair to guess the much-reported delay in releasing the album from Summer to Fall, was probably the result of such ongoing changes. This is a song, the opener after all, that Dylan wanted to get right even as he felt its essence slipping away from him.

CHAPTER 6 / JOKERMAN

7:

License to Kill

Published Lyrics
License to Kill

1   Man thinks 'cause he rules the earth he can do with it as he please

2   And if things don't change soon, he will

3   Oh, man has invented his doom

4   First step was touching the moon

5   Now, there's a woman on my block

6   She just sit there as the night grows still

7   She say who gonna take away his license to kill?

8   Now, they take him and they teach him and they groom him for life

9   And they set him on a path where he's bound to get ill

10   Then they bury him with stars

11   Sell his body like they do used cars

12   Now, there's a woman on my block

13   She just sit there facin' the hill

14   She say who gonna take away his license to kill?

15   Now, he's hell-bent for destruction, he's afraid and confused

16   And his brain has been mismanaged with great skill

17   All he believes are his eyes

18   And his eyes, they just tell him lies

19   But there's a woman on my block

20   Sitting there in a cold chill

21   She say who gonna take away his license to kill?

22   Ya may be a noisemaker, spirit maker

23   Heartbreaker, backbreaker

24   Leave no stone unturned

25   May be an actor in a plot

26   That might be all that you got

27   Til your error you clearly learn

28   Now he worships at an altar of a stagnant pool

29   And when he sees his reflection, he's fulfilled

30   Oh, man is opposed to fair play

31   He wants it all and he wants it his way

32   Now, there's a woman on my block

33   She just sit there as the night grows still

34   She say who gonna take away his license to kill?

Writing

'License to Kill' is a song with a short gestation and an almost blink-and-you miss-it" recording history. Its lyrics are very direct, with only the observation about man's doom stemming from "touching the moon," having any of requisite Dylan vagueness.[116] The song encapsulates the core exploration of *Infidels*, the present-day self-absorbed species and its relationship with the Earth, its brethren and its Lord. Early in the first Notebook are two lines that later branched off into the unreleased 'Julius and Ethel' and give an illustration about where Dylan's thoughts (as written) were during this period: "He might do just as he want but not for as long as he like."[117] A lyric sheet, which is essentially for 'Julius and Ethel', also includes much of lines 28 and 29 above. The difference is the words "he's fulfilled" were "he drinks his fill."[118]

The archive has one lyric sheet for 'License to Kill'. Other than some small changes, the verses are already close to the final lyrics. The final verse is not

---

116 / Some three years later, following the Challenger Space Shuttle disaster, Dylan wrote of that program, "Can't build a tower of Babel, God says 'You don't come here'." He referred to it as "murder in outer space....pioneers chosen to die."
BDA 2016.01 B32 F06.01
117 / BDA Notebook One P 10
118 / BDA 2016.01.B35 F06 04

on the lyric sheet. Dylan also tried another thought about the controlled flow of information and how millions are ruled by so few. The bridge, lines 22-27, originally had a pauper, pilgrim and permanent stranger instead of the noise makers, etc. The released song has man manipulated, as his having internalized what he's been taught and acting robotically. In draft, these manipulations are forcibly directed, up to and including at gunpoint.

The voice presented in the lyrics indicates the influence of Dylan's time in the Caribbean islands. Man "do as he please," rather than, "he pleases." "She just sit," instead of "She just sits." "She say," not "She says."[119]

An interesting aside is provided in the main book accompanying the *Trouble No More* box set.

A page of draft lyrics for 'When You Gonna Wake Up' has the used car/star rhyme combination.[120]

Recording

'License to Kill' was the last song recorded during the April 13 session, otherwise devoted to 'Jokerman'. It was completed in a single take, not counting five seconds of a botched start. The take has a two-beat guitar and drum intro. When released, the guitar intro is mixed out and the drums, loudly pronounced. Mick Taylor plays slide throughout, but it has been mixed out for release, leaving Knopfler's guitar accenting the verses until the end, when it duels with Taylor's slide and with the harmonica. A lovely organ part was also brought up for the release.

There are no obvious overdubs for this one-and-done perfection.

'License to Kill' was an early pick for promotion. Dylan and the musicians were filmed lip-synching the song during the sessions (see Chapter 24). Dylan has an odd hat on for the pantomime. The filming could have been done by Albert and David Maysles[121] who also filmed 90 minutes of silent footage that are part of the archive. These seem to also be acted, as opposed to performed music.

---

119 / Much appreciation to long-time Dylan researcher and chronicler Ian Woodward for pointing out the Island patois

120 / Bob Dylan *Trouble No More* 2017, p. 23

121 / The Maysles brothers were documentarians, probably most famous for *Gimme Shelter* which covered the Rolling Stones disastrous 1969 Altamont, California concert

Dylan performed the song on March 22, 1984, on *The David Letterman Show*. He was backed by what was described as a punk band consisting of guitarist J.J. Holliday, bassist Tony Marisco and drummer Charley Quintana. The performance was bolder and harsher than the superior album version done with superior musicians. Quintana was a second drummer for a few months of a 1992 Dylan tour.

'License to Kill' was in the set-list nightly during the 1984 European Tour and then sporadically up to 1998.

CHAPTER 7 / LICENSE TO KILL

8:

Clean-Cut Kid

Published Lyrics
Clean-Cut Kid

1	Everybody wants to know why he couldn't adjust
2	Adjust to what, a dream that bust?
3	He was a clean-cut kid
4	But they made a killer out of him
5	That's what they did
6	They said what's up is down, they said what isn't is
7	They put ideas in his head he thought were his
8	He was a clean-cut kid
9	But they made a killer out of him
10	That's what they did
11	He was on the baseball team, he was in the marching band
12	When he was ten years old he had a watermelon stand
13	He was a clean-cut kid
14	But they made a killer out of him
15	That's what they did
16	He went to church on Sunday, he was a Boy Scout
17	For his friends he would turn his pockets inside out
18	He was a clean-cut kid
19	But they made a killer out of him
20	That's what they did
21	They said, "Listen boy, you're just a pup"
22	They sent him to a napalm health spa to shape up

23   They gave him dope to smoke, drinks and pills
24   A jeep to drive, blood to spill

25   They said "Congratulations, you got what it takes"
26   They sent him back into the rat race without any brakes

27   He was a clean-cut kid
28   But they made a killer out of him
29   That's what they did

30   He bought the American dream but it put him in debt
31   The only game he could play was Russian roulette

32   He drank Coca-Cola, he was eating Wonder Bread Ate Burger Kings, he
        was well fed

33   He went to Hollywood to see Peter O'Toole
34   He stole a Rolls-Royce and drove it in a swimming pool

35   They took a clean-cut kid
36   And they made a killer out of him
37   That's what they did

38   He could've sold insurance, owned a restaurant or bar
39   Could've been an accountant or a tennis star

40   He was wearing boxing gloves, took a dive one day
41   Off the Golden Gate Bridge into China Bay

42   His mama walks the floor, his daddy weeps and moans
43   They gotta sleep together in a home they don't own

44   They took a clean-cut kid
45   And they made a killer out of him

46   That's what they did

27   Well, everybody's asking why he couldn't adjust
48   All he ever wanted was somebody to trust

49   They took his head and turned it inside out
50   He never did know what it was all about

51   He had a steady job, he joined the choir
52   He never did plan to walk the high wire

53   They took a clean-cut kid
54   And they made a killer out of him
55   That's what they did

Writing

'Clean-Cut Kid' was written for *Infidels,* had five complete takes recorded over two days and was not chosen to be on the album. It had a second life when Carla Olson[122] of the Textones recorded it in 1984. It arose again when Dylan recorded it with Ron Wood on July 26, 1984.

Dylan continued with it during the many studio sessions that put together the 1985 *Empire Burlesque*.

The song was originally titled 'Brooklyn Anthem'. Its subject was portrayed as the most average of stereotypical post-war children who internalized the American culture as presented to them by their parents, teachers and media. The "Kid" either enlists or is drafted and is sent to "a napalm health spa," likely Vietnam. After his service, he "couldn't adjust" and ultimately committed suicide. "They" are responsible for taking this nice boy and making him a killer, partly by "putting ideas in his head he thought were his." These words are a lyrical sibling to "his brain has been mismanaged with great skill," from 'License to Kill'.

A number of people who were present in the studio in 1983 or interacting

122 / Carla Olson appeared in the video for 'Sweetheart Like You', a guitar player substituting for Knopfler

with Dylan and/or others involved have the impression that the inspiration for the "Kid" were the life and/or experiences of Brooklyn-born Don DeVito or his brother, a New York City police officer. A Richard D included in the handwritten draft of the album credits under "And the many others who inspired and help make this album." No records have been found indicating either DeVito served in Vietnam nor did they commit suicide. This reminds us not to embrace Dylan's lyrics literally.

At any rate, Dylan lived through the Vietnam war and saw its effects on young Americans who served. 'Clean-Cut Kid' does not come across as a belated protest, more as a poet's observation of human damage.

There are no indications of this song in any of the Notebook writings. The first line differs from the published lyrics, in "They're asking me," becomes "You ask me." There are no truly radical differences in what he began writing and what he finished. In one draft, "murderer" is used instead of "killer." The biggest change would have been an alternative for the end of the chorus, "Now he ain't got no face, he got to keep it hid."[123]

The kid's activities varied from football to baseball to honor roll to high school news. In his yearbook, "wearing tweed he was voted the most likely to succeed." Sometimes the watermelon stand was at six years old, other times nine or ten. Some versions have the "dope to smoke" augmented with "girls for a thrill." One of his professional opportunities in several drafts was "Bette Midler's accountant."

The kid was sent back into a society he was unprepared to re-enter and advised to "forget about what you've seen." Worse than the "no brakes" of the published lyrics, the same draft puts a "monkey on his back" that sometimes maneuvers around to sit on his lap. His parents feel "betrayed... all they got is a rifle that is German made."

Several pages in these drafts diverge into thoughts about or messages to Merle Haggard and the sadness his songs bring to Dylan. These have no apparent relationship to 'Clean-Cut Kid'.

When Dylan reviewed the lyrics for copyright, he cut "The American Dream of mortgage and debt."[124]

123 / BDA 2016.01. B35 F09.01-04
124 / BDA 2016.01.B24

Recording

The first take of 'Clean-Cut Kid' on April 14 was complete It had a shuffle beat, with accenting that is slightly reminiscent of the Grateful Dead's 'US Blues'. Taylor is upfront with guitar.

This is followed by a one-minute recording for consideration as a punch-in.

The following take was a little bit rougher in terms of vocal and backing. The guitar is not as prominent. The organ is the lead instrument.

Engineers notes indicated that Dylan preferred the first take.

There was at least one other April 14 take of 'Clean Cut Kid' on reel 9, but archival gremlins or digital recording flaws have left that part of the recording blank.

On April 15, after two instrumentals, Dylan tells Dorfsman they are going to do 'Brooklyn Anthem'. First, he has a music box that plays a tinkling 'Smoke Gets in Your Eyes'. Dylan wants this as the beginning music for "Kid" and plays it a few times so that band knows when they should come in. "As soon as it shuts off," he tells Dunbar. He wants the engineers to make it "sound gigantic." The song itself has a 2/4 time bounce. Nice slide work accents the verses. This version has the "most likely to succeed" lyric. The vocal is delivered with slightly less investment than on the two the previous day.

The music box disappears on the next take. The guitar playing sounds as if Chuck Berry snuck into the studio for some of his signature licks. Dylan goes a bit sing-song in the second half of the take while doing his best Johnny Johnson on the piano. It's too bad this style was not pursued further as the beat is more dynamic than the previous takes.

Two instrumental takes at the same tempo allow Dylan to consider how to better treat his vocal. Dylan asks to hear "the other one back." They then go for the final attempt of the song with the same souped-up beat. Clark plays the organ reminiscent of Dave "Baby" Cortez. Dylan still does not seem comfortable with singing it in this style. And that is that for 'Clean Cut Kid' until *Empire Burlesque*.

9:

Man of Peace

Published Lyrics
Man of Peace

1   Look out your window, baby, there's a scene you'd like to catch
2   The band is playing "Dixie," a man got his hand outstretched
3   Could be the Führer
4   Could be the local priest
5   You know sometimes Satan comes as a man of peace

6   He got a sweet gift of gab, he got a harmonious tongue
7   He knows every song of love that ever has been sung
8   Good intentions can be evil
9   Both hands can be full of grease
10   You know that sometimes Satan comes as a man of peace

11   Well, first he's in the background, then he's in the front
12   Both eyes are looking like they're on a rabbit hunt
13   Nobody can see through him
14   No, not even the Chief of Police
15   You know that sometimes Satan comes as a man of peace

16   Well, he catch you when you're hoping for a glimpse of the sun
17   Catch you when your troubles feel like they weigh a ton
18   He could be standing next to you
19   The person that you'd notice least
20   I hear that sometimes Satan comes as a man of peace

21   Well, he can be fascinating, he can be dull
22   He can ride down Niagara Falls in the barrels of your skull
23   I can smell something cooking
24   I can tell there's going to be a feast
25   You know that sometimes Satan comes as a man of peace

26   He's a great humanitarian, he's a great philanthropist
27   He knows just where to touch you, honey, and how you like to be kissed
28   He'll put both his arms around you
29   You can feel the tender touch of the beast
30   You know that sometimes Satan comes as a man of peace

31   Well, the howling wolf will howl tonight, the king snake will crawl
32   Trees that've stood for a thousand years suddenly will fall
33   Wanna get married? Do it now
34   Tomorrow all activity will cease
35   You know that sometimes Satan comes as a man of peace

36   Somewhere Mama's weeping for her blue-eyed boy
37   She's holding them little white shoes and that little broken toy
38   And he's following a star
39   The same one them three men followed from the East
40   I hear that sometimes Satan comes as a man of peace

Writing

'Man of Peace' is classic Dylan railing against the manipulators of vulnerable souls.

Though it is tempting to regard "Satan" in the song as literally being the Devil, evil can exist in human form without being supernatural. It could be the actual Devil. Maybe I'm being fooled.

These verses warn how easily one can be lured, go with the embrace or march in the parade. In the Spring of 1980, Dylan performed a new song that recognized he too had a power that didn't require being used for good: "I can manipulate people as well as anybody...I can persuade people as well as anybody....I can twist the truth as well as anybody."[125] "Man of Peace" opening lines 1 through 4 are

---

125 / 'Ain't Gonna Go To Hell For Anybody' was featured in 29 concerts in April and May and fit nicely with the gospel theme of those shows. In the Winter, completely rewritten verses were fit to the original melody. Except for the chorus warning of "a one-way ticket to burn," the new lyrics seem to reflect on a romantic encounter

somewhat cinematic, evoking black and white footage of an open Mercedes making its way along swastika-festooned streets. It doesn't have to be that level of leader, though. A person can be misled down the road right from the church pulpit.

The Notebooks don't hint of this song. Chris Bowman, skipper of *Water Pearl*, believes Dylan may have been inspired by local anger at an Anglican priest out of St. Vincent whom the residents believed was abusing children. Bequians, according to Bowman, hated the priest. The crew members were talking about it on board when Dylan was sailing with them.[126] Maybe that fed into writing, but Bob wouldn't have needed outside inspiration to put together this kind of song.

There are seven complete additional verses scattered through the three drafts in the archives. For some reason, along with the released verses, four of the other verses were submitted to Dylan for review before submitting for copyright. Bob was quite emphatic that they were not to be included. If these were recorded, as seems likely, they were cut from what purports to be the session tapes.[127]

Is the Man of Peace "the same spirit" as the Jokerman? In places both songs seem to arise out of the reflection on the world's susceptibility to "manipulators of crowds" and "dream twisters." One partial draft of 'Man of Peace' has a title "rape on Sunday... robin hood in Miami lone Ranger in japan." After verse three, there is a verse that belongs with 'Jokerman'. Maybe Dylan just made use of a handy sheet of paper. Or maybe the two songs are part of the same group of thoughts.

Those looking for biographical elements can find one when "Mama" hold up "them little white shoes." In the transcript of a 1968 interview with Dylan's parents, Mrs Zimmerman talked to author Robert Shelton of two-year-old Bobby's white shoes.[128] The line in 'Man of Peace' could be an image independent

---

126 / Interview with Chris Bowman. 127. BDA 20.16. B24.F11
127 / The instruction from Dylan was "Forget about it...lose them."
128 / "When he'd see me polishing the white shoes, he was ready to go out." Barker, Derek *Isis: A Bob Dylan Anthology*, (London, 2001). p.16.
Shelton's September 29, 1961, *New York Times* article of a Dylan coffee house appearance led to the 20-year-old's signing by Columbia Records. Shelton's biography, intended originally for the mid-late Sixties, was published in 1986

of personal history. Or it could be a tease, as could be, "he's following a star/the same one them three men followed from the East." One draft verse has the tempter luring his target to a "house of mirrors." Later, like Don Corleone in *The Godfather*, "he's got an offer that you can't refuse." Odd historical figures like Socrates and Cochise and the Birdman of Alcatraz all make appearances.

In the second to last verse, Dylan suggests the end of time, a concept he visits again in 1998s *Time Out of Mind* 's 'Can't Wait'. In 'Man of Peace', the signs of doom in line 31 recall two of Dylan's blues influences: John Lee Hooker's "Crawlin' King Snake" and Howlin' Wolf.

After some intense writing, Dylan likely felt he'd captured the spirit of the song and was satisfied after the three drafts and took the song into the studio.

Recording

'Man of Peace' was recorded on April 14, 1983, interrupting work on 'Clean-Cut Kid', which would be revisited and finished on the 15th. There is one complete take of 'Man of Peace', but the initial take begins with the chorus following the first verse, including a verse about marching up an alley, then an aisle, a saxophone, the Birdman of Alcatraz and the body of Cochise. It's an intriguing verse but comes off as poetic window-dressing and does not advance the theme of evil manipulation. It seems as if the recording was simply to try out that verse, because the taping is stopped shortly after those words are delivered. After 20 seconds playing with the intro, the "Great" take is put down, overdubbed later, kept, becomes the opener for the second side (Remember vinyl?) of *Infidels*. It is an excellent example of rock 'n' roll Dylan. "Marching down the alley" is an appropriate description.

Dylan played 'Man of Peace' in 41 concerts between 1984 and 2000. While it never was a staple in any year, it was played three times in the 1987 *Dylan and the Dead* performances. In rehearsals for that series of shared bills, a Bo Diddley beat propelled the song.

The next session day, April 15, seemed to tax Dylan's energies, and he quickly finished up 'Clean-Cut Kid', jammed and played bits of covers.

CHAPTER 9 / MAN OF PEACE

10:

Someone's Got a Hold of My Heart

Published Lyrics
Someone's Got a Hold of My Heart-

1	They say, "Eat, drink and be merry
2	Take the bull by the horns"
3	I keep seeing visions of you, a lily among thorns
4	Everything looks a little far away to me
5	Gettin' harder and harder to recognize the trap
6	Too much information about nothin'
7	Too much educated rap
8	It's just like you told me, just like you said it would be
9	The moon rising like wildfire
10	I feel the breath of a storm
11	Something I got to do tonight
12	You go inside and stay warm
13	Someone's got a hold of my heart
14	Someone's got a hold of my heart
15	Someone's got a hold of my heart
16	You—
17	Yeah, you got a hold of my heart
18	Just got back from a city of flaming red skies
19	Everybody thinks with their stomach
20	There's plenty of spies
21	Every street is crooked, they just wind around till they disappear
22	Madame Butterfly, she lulled me to sleep
23	Like an ancient river
24	So wide and deep
25	She said, "Be easy, baby, ain't nothin' worth stealin' here"

26   You're the one I've been waitin' for
27   You're the one I desire
28   But you must first realize
29   I'm not another man for hire

30   Someone's got a hold of my heart
31   Someone's got a hold of my heart
32   Someone's got a hold of my heart
33   You, you, you, you
34   Yeah, you got a hold of my heart

35   Hear that hot-blooded singer
36   On the bandstand croon
37   September song, Memphis in June
38   While they're beating the devil out of a guy who's wearing a powder Íblue wig

39   I been to Babylon
40   I gotta confess
41   I could still hear the voice crying in the wilderness
42   What looks large from a distance, close up is never that big
43   Never could learn to drink that blood and call it wine
44   Never could learn to look at your face and call it mine

45   Someone's got a hold of my heart
46   Someone's got a hold of my heart
47   Someone's got a hold of my heart
48   You—
49   Yeah, you got a hold of my heart

Writing

'Tight Connection to My Heart(Has Anybody Seen My Love)' on *Empire Burlesque*, *Infidels* 1985 successor, grew directly from the earlier album's outtakes of 'Someone's Got A Hold of My Heart'. 'Someone's' is a song that began with and evolved from a great deal of complexity. Dylan devoted much effort on focusing the story and refining the lyrics. It is not surprising that he kept reworking it even after it was not selected for the album for which it was first written.

On the very first page of the January 1983 Notebook,[129] believed to be from a *Water Pearl* sail, the second line is "I was telling myself 'Ain't nothing worth stealing in here.'" This changes within one page to Madame Butterfly (line 22), who tells him the same thing. Two pages later, he writes "never could drink blood and call it wine."

As Dylan progresses with his word play for what became the song, he portrays Madame Butterfly as a subject of sexual desire, "knowing I'd have to be an acrobat." She dispenses the "be easy baby" advice that is part of the final lyrics. Thoughts of unsettled weather (line 10) come to the writer: "something in the air tonight, go inside and stay warm (line 12); "a sign of a storm"(line 10). A Notebook page later, he writes "wild fire... I feel the breath of a storm" are written.

Dylan was still playing with the Madame Butterfly concept 16 pages into the Notebook, where there are also several references to goat's head soup (Jamaican cuisine, not the Rolling Stones' record album) and perhaps to its potential as an aphrodisiac.

Lyrics show an island influence predating his January writing. Draft lyrics refer to Babylon. While there are Old and New Testament connections with a Babylon (and in Dylan's own 'Neighborhood Bully'), the context of this song indicates a Rastafarian meaning.[130] Dylan would have commonly heard references to Babylon repeated conversation and in reggae lyrics in the Caribbean.[131] Ancient Babylon was a conqueror, exiler and representative of evil on earth. The Rasta culture arose in the Thirties among the descendants of the African slaves in Jamaica (coinciding with Italian dictator Mussolini's aggression against Ethiopia). Ethiopia's Emperor, Haile Selassie, was a saintly figure, even a deity,

---

129 / BDA Notebook One

130 / At the time of the *New Testament*, Babylon had ceased to be a power. But "Babylon" was used to symbolize great evil. In the *Book of Revelations*, Babylon is referred to as "the Great Whore." Dylan would have been familiar with this from Bible study and reading, including "Upon her forehead was a name written 'Mystery, Babylon the Great, the Mother of Harlots." Dylan used this image in his final lyrics for 'Foot of Pride

131/ /Barrett, Leonard. E Sr., Leonard E. Barrett Sr. *The Rastafarians: The Twentieth Anniversary Edition*, (Beacon Press, Boston), 1997

in the Rasta belief system. The slave trade led to an African diaspora almost interchangeably called Babylon or a disaster caused by Babylon. At any rate, Babylon was a concept and location in opposition to righteous Rastas.

Rastafarianism has at its core the rejection of Babylon, which is the earthly manifestation of all evil, including exile and enslavement.

It appears that the subsequent Notebook jottings were thoughts for revising the song for which Dylan had already done 10 drafts. None of the drafts have Madame Butterfly, the suggestion to "be easy," storm conditions, or the blood/wine distinction.

The title and chorus, 'Someone's Got A Hold of My Heart' were present from the beginning, but the scenario was quite different.[132] In the various drafts, the narrator was either reflecting on or searching for the reason he could not sleep at night. There is a persistent light, an undefined vision, the sound of bells or of a distant train. Everything looks "a little far away." His path is blocked by a bolt of lightning, keeping him from deciding his direction. He feels he should be able to choose because he's taught others well but now must learn for himself.

Earlier approaches to the thoughts in lines 5 and 6 have him "running into newsboys selling yesterday's news." But all this was predicted, "just like you said it would be." The observation "nothing worth stealing in here" is delivered by a stranger or someone yelling down. Whatever has caused this restlessness—a departed lover, a change in how he views the world—is not clear from the lyrics. Whatever the cause, he has changed: what he used to see as straight now seems crooked. A familiar melody is just out of reach. It seems at its essence to be "you, you, you, you, you got a hold of my heart."

In the second draft's verse, the narrator has just returned from: "a place so white," "a city painted red," "a place (city or planet) called night," "a place so alone," "a battle zone." While the crooked streets of the published lyrics are in one draft, they are contrasted by "every head is square." Along the path, the store windows are broken. His nerves are "running like milk white steeds."[133] While he seems lost at present, he confesses having been to Babylon or, in one version, it's "the lost city." While the writing resolves with Line 41's "voice crying

132. 2016.0 BDA 1.B35.F07.1-10
133. See Jokerman, line 30

in the wilderness," in another draft, he could not discern between "brutality and tenderness." The caution about the true size of things seen from a distance is consistent in the drafts, perhaps tying in with the first verse "everything looks a little far away." Some of the drafts of the second verse include a person who "kept mistaking me for a friend." That character has "long golden reddish hair and icicles for teeth."

The song the narrator hears in verse four, "September Song, Memphis In June," is delivered by the "hot-blooded singer" of Line 35 as well as by humming banjoes and crooning saxophones. Or, perhaps, he's hearing an "old Hoagy Carmichael tune." At the same time, the smell of bar-b- cued pig is blocking his breathing. The image of the man in the powder blue wig having the devil beaten out of him is in most drafts (Line 38). The published ending about drinking blood and calling it wine is not found in any of the non-notebook work.

Dylan wrote scores of words for this three-verse plus chorus song. He wrote, and wrote some more. He let his thoughts run when on his boat and injected them into the lyrics he took to the studio. As shown above, the song he recorded dispensed with the "I can't sleep" opening in favor of one of the many clichés on *Infidels*: "Eat, Drink, and Be Merry."

When Dylan's office put together lyrics for his review for publishing purposes, Line 10 was transcribed as "I feel the breath of a skunk." Bob's understandable reaction was "What! (Storm)."[134]

Recording

The initial April 16 recordings of 'Someone's Got A Hold of My Heart' are instrumentals as Dylan and the musicians seek a comfort zone with the chord changes and rhythm. From time to time, Dylan seems to have a problem finding the proper fret on his guitar as he switches back and forth from chording to picking out notes.[135] Taylor, Shakespeare and Dunbar play with no evident difficulty. In a six-and-a-half-minute run-through, the repetitive licks become reminiscent of The Riviera's 1964 'California Sun'. Two takes exceed six minutes. For the first, Clark is on organ, for the second, piano. After seven of these

---

134. BDA 2016.01.B25.F06
135 / It is possible that Dylan's guitar was an overdub attempt, as it sounds like Dylan on piano as well

rehearsals are committed to tape, none with vocals, the song is set aside for nine days. It's possible Dylan wanted the music with him back at his hotel as he worked on the lyrics.

On April 25, an electric piano played by Clark is prominent as vocals are introduced. On the first take, Dylan does a gentle vocal, obviously not intended to be a keeper. Dylan provides some instructions, followed by two false starts. Dylan muses about finding a new studio "where they don't have trees," and then records the version of the song that is on *The Bootleg Series Vol. 1-3*. Vocal overdubs are added later, and extraneous harmonica is removed.

The following day, a more up-tempo version is recorded with two false starts and two complete versions, with Dylan again trying his guitar picking. There are no harmonica breaks on these versions. The second complete version began circulating in 1984 via a bootleg tape. It was the only known version of the song until 1991.

'Someone's Got A Hold of My Heart' is a good song, although as *Infidels* came together as an album during the month of recording, it may have seemed too upbeat to be included. The three sessions worth of work did not go to waste, as Dylan kept the backing track and reworked the words for Empire Burlesque. That 1985 album had a number of songs with a more positive view toward subjects like love.[136]

136 / These include 'Emotionally Yours', 'I'll Remember You' and "Never Gonna be the Same Again'

11:

Sweetheart Like You

Published Lyrics
Sweetheart Like You

1   Well, the pressure's down, the boss ain't here

2   He gone North, he ain't around

3   They say that vanity got the best of him

4   But he sure left here after sundown

5   By the way, that's a cute hat

6   And that smile's so hard to resist

7   But what's a sweetheart like you doin' in a dump like this?

8   You know, I once knew a woman who looked like you

9   She wanted a whole man, not just a half

10   She used to call me sweet daddy when I was only a child

11   You kind of remind me of her when you laugh

12   In order to deal in this game, got to make the queen disappear

13   It's done with a flick of the wrist

14   What's a sweetheart like you doin' in a dump like this?

15   You know, a woman like you should be at home

16   That's where you belong

17   Watching out for someone who loves you true

18   Who would never do you wrong

19   Just how much abuse will you be able to take?

20   Well, there's no way to tell by that first kiss

21   What's a sweetheart like you doin' in a dump like this?

22   You know you can make a name for yourself

23   You can hear them tires squeal

24   You can be known as the most beautiful woman

25   Who ever crawled across cut glass to make a deal

26   You know, news of you has come down the line

27   Even before ya came in the door
28   They say in your father's house, there's many mansions
29   Each one of them got a fireproof floor
30   Snap out of it, baby, people are jealous of you
31   They smile to your face, but behind your back they hiss
32   What's a sweetheart like you doin' in a dump like this?

33   Got to be an important person to be in here, honey
34   Got to have done some evil deed
35   Got to have your own harem when you come in the door
36   Got to play your harp until your lips bleed

37   They say that patriotism is the last refuge
38   To which a scoundrel clings
39   Steal a little and they throw you in jail
40   Steal a lot and they make you king
41   There's only one step down from here, baby
42   It's called the land of permanent bliss
43   What's a sweetheart like you doin' in a dump like this?

Writing

It is disappointing that are no draft lyrics for 'Sweetheart Like You' in the Archives.

Perhaps the song was completely composed in the studio, but one would expect at least a handwritten working copy on legal paper. There is nothing. Nada. Just a mystery.

On page twelve of the notebook begun in January 1983, there are some lines that make their way into the song: "got to have done some worthless deed," "permanent bliss; it's here all right, it's called the land of." In fact, "permanent bliss" is written on two different lines on the page. Nothing else relates to the finished song, except perhaps a reference to cards. On page 15 are more phrases Dylan plays with during recording. "I'll give your compliments to the chef if he hasn't gone to the land of permanent bliss." He mentions a "price that don't exist," which in some takes is the rhyme for "this" in the third verse.

The song seems like a bar-room encounter with the same one-way discourse presented in "'Tell Me.' In 'Sweetheart', the person doing all the talking seems to be doing all he can to convince a woman that she's not seeing her life clearly. Compliments, "that's a cute hat," comparisons, "I once knew a woman who looked like you...you kinda remind me of her," incredulity, "how much abuse will you be able to take?" and warning "only one step down from here," seem to be an odd manner of seduction. Whether the attempt is to provide a general spiritual warning, or to possess the woman's body or soul is an open question. At any rate, it demonstrates a sweet gift of gab.

In 'Tell Me', discussed in Chapter 13, there is already a relationship but not a very long or deep one. The contrast between that song and 'Sweetheart' is that in 'Sweetheart', the narrator does the telling. In 'Tell Me', he's seeking answers.

Dylan received criticism from self-identified feminists for the third verse. Dylan offered a rare and muted mea culpa when talking with Kurt Loder in 1984: "Actually, that line didn't come out exactly the way I wanted it to. But, uh . . . I could easily have changed that line to make it not so overly, uh, tender, you know? But I think the concept still woulda been the same. You see a fine-lookin' woman walking down the street, you start goin,' "Well, what are you doin' on the street? You're so fine, what do you need all this for?"[137]

Recording

'Sweetheart Like You', "musically one of the prettiest compositions on *Infidels*, is the best illustration of one of the different ways session's songs came together. Like 'Jokerman', like 'Don't Fall Apart on Me Tonight', the recordings of the song in the archives, including run tapes, evidence of a work in progress. In the studio, 'Sweetheart' was worked on for over three hours. Knopfler at one point says "It's different than when you played it at my place the other night," indicating that Dylan prepared the producer for this and other songs before the recording process. On April 16, Knopfler, Clark and Mick on slide dobro play several sweet minutes of 'People Get Ready', and its melody influences some early treatments of 'Sweetheart'.

137 / *Bob Dylan: Recovering Christian*, Kurt Loder Rolling Stone, June 21, 1984

There are 26 digital takes[138] of this song on April 18 .[139] And there are about 10 more that are only on two of the run tapes documenting this day.[140] Some are complete. Many are false starts or last no more than two minutes. A couple are instrumentals. Other than the album take, no recording earns the conclusion "they nailed it—that's where they should have stopped." That can be said about take four of 15 for 'Like a Rolling Stone'. Not in this case. One take in the middle of two session reels from April 18 is closest to the finished song. The vocal is practically complete and much of the music is what forms the final version. This was likely the "Master" take, which Josh Abbey would describe as "a long way from the album master at this point." Its designation indicates it is the "choice multitrack onto which dubs could be added at any time—on the day of recording or thereafter."

The first hour in the studio was nearly all instrumental as the musicians developed the feel, key and chords. As Dylan began faintly singing the words 50 minutes in, the search for the key took on urgency as the music was pitched too high in some run throughs. One particular vexing problem was the chord underneath "dump like this." Initially, it mirrored the music under "thank the Lord" on 'People Get Ready'. Halfway into the second hour, Robbie simply stayed on an A, and that was the solution.[141]

Dylan occasionally displayed frustration, "This song is giving me trouble. I don't know why. Feels so ordinary, though." Later, he remarked, "These ballads are a bitch. They get harder and harder every year. Gee, Mick, how you doing, Mick are you still here...There's a tension to it that's not there. A tense part that's not in it." Knopfler suggested, "I think it needs to be more intimate." Bob replied,

138 / Determined from listening to the tapes

139 / Michael Krogsgaard did pioneering research into all of Dylan's sessions through 1991. He has stated that 'Sweetheart' was begun on April 14 in two takes. The song is not on the tape reel (9), and the written record for this song and 'Clean Cut Kid' is marked "not here." If it was recorded on the 14th, maybe Dylan had it wiped. In fact, when working on 'Sweetheart' on April 18, he tells Dorfsman, "You can roll over all this stuff," and then asks about 'Clean Cut Kid' "from the other night."

140 / About 18 minutes of the second of three run tapes was bootlegged several years later. Ironically, this tape did not match any material on the session recordings. That fact, combined with the engineers writing things like "Run #1," led to the further search, discovery and addition of the run tapes to the archives

141 Some of the third run tape reel includes a number of playbacks of a track late in the second run tape. This take was subsequently overdubbed and is take 16 on Reel 16

"I do too, but it's got to be set up that way. You can't just do it, it's got to be set up. But the more set up it is, the more intimate it can be."

Knopfler earned his producer credit with this song, constantly encouraging, "You guys sound beautiful....Feels great, feels great, feels great...It's gonna be great (to which Dylan said, "Yeah, I can see that." Mark stayed in charge, "Gonna be great, man. Don't blow it now." Bob said, "Ok."

At one point, Dylan remarked, "It sounds like a Nashville arrangement, like a cocktail thing? Yeah, but you hear glasses tinkling and blue lights and stuff like that. It creates a mood. We're not doing that mood." Knopfler immediately suggested Clark play cocktail style, "more lounge style." He instructed Dylan to sing low and close into the mic, "nice and easy and gentle." Knopfler also suggested several times that Bob not play guitar.

During the same time the music was slowly being developed, Dylan searched for lyrics to add to the parts of the song he was committed to. Variations abound on session recordings.

Dylan's go-to opening line was, "The pressure's down," but sometimes the boss was gone. In one, the lights were out. While the published lyrics state, "he ain't around...he left here after sundown," the album tells us, "he gone North for awhile...he sure left here in style." In some takes, he's gone "to that lighthouse around the bend...he didn't trust no one in the end." Maybe one of his musicians said something about pressure drop, as Dylan says, "'Pressure Drop's' been done."[142]

For a few takes, the chairman of the board is not present: he's "caught the red eye and it left on time." In one version, "he (the boss) wants to avoid that Moonlight Mile."[143] On his way out, the last thing he says is, "See ya' later," and wherever he's going, "he's starting a graveyard there."

Very early in the session, Dylan tried, "Well the pressure's down, but the keys have been misplaced/Door on the right is locked/and the other's in your face."

Dylan was pretty consistent with the somewhat offhand hat compliment, although in one take the compliment is on a pair of boots that are "cute."

142 'Pressure Drop' was recorded in Jamaica in 1969 by Toots and the Maytals and covered by many.
143 'Moonlight Mile' was a song on the Rolling Stones *Sticky Fingers* album for which Mick Taylor may have been led to believe he would get a writing credit. Perhaps Bob was being as cute as the hat with this particular variation

The second verse appears to have been more problematic before the narrator ultimately compares the current woman to one in the past. Elsewhere in the sessions, he had taken his "clothes to Red River to be washed." More interesting to the warning as seduction concept is, "You know con men don't meet strangers, to them there are none. In a quarter of an hour they're good friends with everyone." In working with the rhythmic flow of the lines, Dylan tries, "Caught him with no strangers, caught him with a lie/One harem on Sunday morning, one on Saturday night." Then Dylan settled in lyrically on getting to the flick of the wrist and sometimes sang about dealing from the bottom of the deck.

For lines 19 and 20, some attempts included, "I see you there across the room/ and an endless thought persists," "You look to me like royalty, etc."

The first bridge was locked down from the start. The next verse continued the work in progress characteristic of this session. The candidate for lines 26-31, up until overdubs, talked about oppression, injustice and misplaced trust. On April 18, some of the lines included, "Five bits can eat your heart out/but you have to give your mind away first." The second bridge only changed in characterizing the required deed as being dirty, lowdown dirty or worthless—before settling on evil.

The thoughts and lyrics of 'Sweetheart Like You' are consistent throughout about an absent authority figure. (Decades later, in 'Ain't Talkin', "the gardener is gone" from the garden.) Also, a compliment about a "cute" article of clothing was certainly a conversation starter based on a most superficial observation. The first bridge (lines 22-25) offered a path to fame and the effort required. The second bridge (lines 33-36) showed what happens after reaching for the gold ring. The final verse may or may not have been the point of the song or an important observation Dylan was determined to deliver, including what awaits at the path's end and Samuel Johnson's quote on patriotism.

The track sheet that accompanies this recording documents live tracks and assigns tracks for instrument and vocal overdubs. It indicates what parts came from among the 32 tracks and were bounced into a composite track.[144] The lovely solo Taylor plays at the end is the product of this composition process, as are Knopfler's parts. Much of this could have occurred on April 18 but certainly

144 / Email correspondence with Josh Abbey March 30, 2019

would have been done before Knopfler's departure May 5. Overdub sessions in May, June and July may have included more tinkering.

The whole production process of 'Sweetheart Like You' and other, but not all, *Infidels* songs and outtakes, according to Abbey, "illustrates how talented people use trial-and-error and then make good decisions!"

12:

Neighborhood Bully

Published Lyrics
Neighborhood Bully

1   Well, the neighborhood bully, he's just one man
2   His enemies say he's on their land
3   They got him outnumbered about a million to one
4   He got no place to escape to, no place to run
5   He's the neighborhood bully

6   The neighborhood bully just lives to survive
7   He's criticized and condemned for being alive
8   He's not supposed to fight back, he's supposed to have thick skin
9   He's supposed to lay down and die when his door is kicked in
10 He's the neighborhood bully

11 The neighborhood bully been driven out of every land
12 He's wandered the earth an exiled man
13 Seen his family scattered, his people hounded and torn
14 He's always on trial for just being born
15 He's the neighborhood bully

16 Well, he knocked out a lynch mob, he was criticized
17 Old women condemned him, said he should apologize.
18 Then he destroyed a bomb factory, nobody was glad
19 The bombs were meant for him. He was supposed to feel bad
20 He's the neighborhood bully

21 Well, the chances are against it and the odds are slim
22 That he'll live by the rules that the world makes for him
23 Cause there's a noose at his neck and a gun at his back
24 And a license to kill him is given out to every maniac
25 He's the neighborhood bully

26   He got no allies to really speak of
27   What he gets he must pay for, he don't get it out of love
28   He buys obsolete weapons and he won't be denied
29   But no one sends flesh and blood to fight by his side
30   He's the neighborhood bully

31   Well, he's surrounded by pacifists who all want peace
32   They pray for it nightly that the bloodshed must cease
33   Now, they wouldn't hurt a fly. To hurt one they would weep
34   They lay and they wait for this bully to fall asleep
35   He's the neighborhood bully

36   Every empire that's enslaved him is gone
37   Egypt and Rome, even the great Babylon
38   He's made a garden of paradise in the desert sand
39   In bed with nobody, under no one's command
40   He's the neighborhood bully

41   Now his holiest books have been trampled upon
42   No contract he signed was worth what it was written on
43   He took the crumbs of the world and he turned it into wealth
44   Took sickness and disease and he turned it into health
45   He's the neighborhood bully

46   What's anybody indebted to him for?
47   Nothin', they say. He just likes to cause war
48   Pride and prejudice and superstition indeed
49   They wait for this bully like a dog waits to feed
50   He's the neighborhood bully

51   What has he done to wear so many scars?
52   Does he change the course of rivers? Does he pollute the moon and stars?
53   Neighborhood bully, standing on the hill

54   Running out the clock, time standing still
55   Neighborhood bully

Writing

'Neighborhood Bully' is the hardest rocking song on *Infidels*. Yes, 'Union Sundown' plows loudly ahead in its own way, but not in the same straight-ahead way of 'Bully'. Had it survived the cut, 'Julius and Ethel', the only unpublished original from the sessions, would have joined 'Bully' in beat and spirit. 'Julius and Ethel' will be discussed in Chapter 17. Both songs seem to have arisen from a reflection on the relationship between Jews and the world. The concept of scapegoating and its irrational isolating unfairness seem to be the foundation of both songs.

'Neighborhood Bully' has had many critics at release, and even today. In *The New York Times*, which usually delights in Dylan releases, Stephen Holden claimed in 1983, "The lyrics suggest an angry crackpot throwing wild punches and hoping that one or two will land."[145] Encyclopedist Michael Gray in a review in *The Telegraph*, used phrases like "self-imitation" and "numb the listener with tedium."[146]

Most contemporaneous objections centered around what was characterized as a perceived uncritical support of Israel and its policies. Nearly 40 years later, the song is cited as viewed through a glass distorted by decades of increasingly effective public relations for a Palestinian viewpoint. This paints every Israeli military action and government policy as fascist, apartheid-like and anti-human rights. However, Dylan, who had made a number of trips to Israel, was not writing on West Bank settlements, border walls, or the like. The song lays out the plight of the Jewish people throughout history and loudly asks the question "Why?" He also presents the vigilance Israel, as well as Jews throughout the world, must practice to keep at bay the enslavers, bomb makers, hypocrites, murderers and those who "lay and wait" for the guard to be let down, to "fall asleep."

Dylan, whether following Christianity or returning to his "roots," was Jewish. His family, many of his friends and those with whom he studied in Brooklyn

145 / Holden, Stephen *Bob Dylan Mingles Exhilaration and Misanthropy. The New York Times*, November 13, 1983 pp. 21, 24

146 / Gray, Michael *Infidelity. The Telegraph*, Manchester, UK, Summer 1984, p. 61

would have influenced this portion of his inherited identity. He may have taken from recent history that, whatever his professed beliefs, he would be viewed as a Jew by anyone wanting to discriminate or even perpetrate another Holocaust. Whether he could have foreseen the increasing spread of antisemitism, and a tolerance for it, in the 21st century is a reach.

The song can be seen as a scorching argument of the right for a people to exist. That this right was embodied within the borders of a state was a fact of history at the time the lyrics were written. The State actions personified a people determined to exist.

Dylan has never performed 'Neighborhood Bully' in concert, even in Israel where many were aching for it to be sung. Research fails to show any record of statements by Dylan about Israeli or Palestinian politics. In the June 1984 *Rolling Stone* interview with Kurt Loder, he was cynical about peace in general, "the time it takes to reload the gun," but this was a commentary on mankind. We might speculate where his heart lies, but unless he has buried it deeply in metaphor in subsequent writings, this is the limit of what he has had to say.

'Neighborhood Bully' was not a song written to fill space on an album.

There is a hint that Dylan was thinking about the topic the song on page 10 of the first notebook. Further down the page are lines that cropped up in 'Julius and Ethel:' "He might do just as he want, but not for as long as he like."[147]

As for the written lyrics, a line that does not fit with anything else is on the reverse of a sheet with 'Tell Me' lyric possibilities. That line is: "What has he done to anyone to breed such hate."[148]

Dylan worked on the ideas further, writing on an index card, "What he done to anybody, well that's hard to say." He concluded with, "he exists that's enough." In the end, "he's" criticized for being alive. The underlying prejudices against "him" are fanned by "one-sided press reports." As he works out ideas, Dylan references the desert sand, "way down in Egypt land," and "Let My People go."[149]

On the next written entry, he works on a vision of "wandering the earth,"

---

147 / One can make too much of notebook jottings. On one page is a curious list: "chocolate ghost truffle, jumbo elephant nose, pink kissing angel, and african devil."
These turn out to be species of tropical fish
148 / BDA, 2016.01.B35. F05.02
149 / BDA, 2016.01.B35.F06.01

scattered family, perpetually at war, buying support and only wanting to exist. On a succeeding draft, Dylan references the Entebbe rescue, where "he" went deep into enemy territory to rescue family only to be criticized.[150]

A fifth draft has line 42 and the "one-man, back to the wall" words not yet part of any verse: 'He's got his back to the wall at the edge of the world/There is no place to fall."

The song goes through five more progressions, with trial verses and an edited word or two. Some of the lines left on the cutting room floor include one dealing with "his" being shot at just for sport; living and hiding like a monk; being the only one sober in a party of drunks; watching others fight to conquer or resist, while "he" fights to exist; the short memory of the world; being on "the firing line of a terrorist game," it's a kill or be killed situation and, finally, makes a last stand in a malarial swamp. The pinnacle of Dylan's outrage is in one of his most direct comments in years: "The world's got a double standard/that's what I think.......A big bunch of hypocrites who all smell like a rose/who wouldn't know the truth if it bit off their nose.[151]"

The composition effort for the song is not linear by any means. Drafts are interrupted by an attempted song about Bob Marley, some more 'Julius and Ethel' lines, pondering on "Stardust" and "Stormy Weather" and "they're alright I guess." Finally, there is an ongoing rant about a *Rolling Stone* critic.

By April 19, Dylan had crafted the lyrics, and was ready for recording.

Recording

After spending a lot of time writing, Dylan recorded 'Neighborhood Bully" fairly quickly. The April 19 work was completed in slightly over one hour. There are short sections recorded to get a feel for the song, and Bob says "This is my song I dedicate to The Clash." Still playing with lyrics, the bully is "just one man, out of the fire into the frying pan." He takes a little time to communicate to the band

---

150 / On July 4, 1976, Israeli Defense Forces flew 2500 miles into Uganda to rescue 94 Jewish passengers and 12 members of the Air France flight crew. They had been held for a week on a plane, flying from Tel Aviv to Paris, hijacked by members of the Popular Front for the Liberation of Palestine. There was a post-rescue effort in the United Nations Security Council to condemn the "Israeli aggression," and Henry Kissinger objected to Israel's use of U.S. equipment
151 / BDA 2016.01.B35.F06.08

how he wants them to play. On the run tape, there are brief experiments with different rhythms and drum parts, and some distress from Dylan that he couldn't hear himself well. Within five minutes of seriously recorded work, a complete take is laid down, with the "shot at for sport" and "sober at the party" lyrics included. There is some wonderful guitar and piano work on this take. The second take becomes the master with six guitar parts, including slide and overdubs from Mick Taylor to choose from. An almost continual harmonica overdub is on one of the 32 tracks. On May 17, there was an overdub session where Ron Wood lay down a part. This take also has a version with a horn section, which may also have occurred on May 17, but was just as possibly recorded on July 7. Somewhere in the process, the Farfisa was dubbed onto the multitracks. A third take had been completed on April 19th, and included handclaps (real or machine?) lyrical variations and an overdubbed bass part. A healthy amount of presence was provided for Dylan's vocal on the final album mix.

Not surprisingly, the song found more of a warm reception in Israel. In 2012, Ariel Zilber released a version in Hebrew on his album *Anabel*.

13:

Tell Me

Published Lyrics
Tell Me

1   Tell me--I've got to know

2   Tell me--tell me before I go

3   Does that flame still burn, Does that fire still glow

4   Or has it died out and melted like the snow

5   Tell me

6   Tell me

7   Tell me--what are you focused upon

8   Tell me--will it come to me after you're gone

9   Tell me quick with a glance on the side

10 Shall I hold you close or shall I let you go by

11 Tell me

12 Tell me

13 Are you lookin' at me and thinking of somebody else

14 Can you feel the heat and the beat of my pulse

15 Do you have any secrets

16 That will only come out in time

17 Do you lay in bed and stare at the stars

18 Is your main friend someone who's an old acquaintance of ours

19 Tell me

20 Tell me

21 Tell me--what's in back of them pretty brown eyes

22 Tell me--behind what door your treasure lies

23 Ever gone broke in a big way

24 Ever done the opposite of what the experts say

25 Tell me

26 Tell me

27   Is it some kind of game that you're playin' with me
28   Am I imagining something that never can be
29   Do you have any morals
30   Do you have any point of view
31   Is that a smile I see on your face
32   Will it take you to glory or to disgrace
33   Tell me
34   Tell me

35   Tell me--is my name in your book
36   Tell me--will you go back and take another look

37   Tell me the truth, tell me no lies
38   Are you someone whom anyone prays for or cries
39   Tell me
40   Tell me

Writing

'Tell Me' seems a progression from the one-sided conversation in 'Sweetheart Like You'. In 'Sweetheart', the speaker tells the woman things she may or may not realize regarding herself of dangers in her path. In this song, the dynamic has flipped with a badgering series of questions: "Tell me, I've got to know." Now that he's made his pitch, he wants to know if he's making any kind of connection with her. There's an indication of initial success: "Does that flame still burn?" He wants to know what kind of woman she is—is she a romantic, is she easy, is she bold? He also wants to know how forward he should be, "Should I hold you close or let you go by?"

There's a bit of desperation when he asks, "Do you have any morals, do you have any point of view?" (The lack of response echoes the experience many have related about trying to get Dylan to answer questions).

At the end, he reverts to playing on possible insecurities she may have "Are you anyone someone cares for or cries?"

On page seven of the first notebook, the idea of telling things someone doesn't need to know, which is used in some drafts of "Too Late/Foot of Pride," is one idea among lines about parasites and deception. On the next page, Dylan gets to, "Tell me-oh tell me (now) I need to know." There's a mention of "dead lion" and "old ship of Zion," words used in one of the compiled master takes but not the one chosen for publication.

Notebook writings indicate that at least the idea for 'Tell Me' was gestating and may have split off at some developmental point from 'Someone's Got A Hold Of My Heart'. Or, the pages were simply filled with lyrical possibilities to be plugged in at a later appropriate point.

By page 22, an entire notebook page is filled with potential lyrics, briefly including the likelihood of the man and woman having already met, but mostly pointing toward an initial feeling out: "what kind of games you have in your mind."

When he gets around to writing and typing out lyrics, Dylan has a seemingly endless set of questions for the woman and, once more, indicates that this is not a first-time encounter. "Tell me," he implores, "am I losing you once (again)/ can I no longer call you my friend." Other questions demonstrate Bob's wordplay in writing his songs: "is there someone you're trying to replace; do you easily change your mind; who you'd like me to be; do you change your mind real fast; do you see anything in me; if my love for you will do; is it too early or too late; how much do you weigh; is that the real face that you wear; "do you think of yourself as someone's plaything or toy/are you like a waitress who says 'what'll it be boy?'"

The "heat and beat of my pulse" line(14) is mostly lifted and transplanted from the published 'Tell Me' lyrics into the 1984 Brussels rewrite of 'Tangled Up In Blue'.

All of his questions are somewhat like "getting to know you, getting to know all about you."[152] As his desire pushes him forward, his heart holds him back: "I don't like playing with fire just to get burned."

'Tell Me" was side by side with 'Someone's Got A Hold of My Heart' on the first Bootleg Series release, hinting that they were part of the same narrative flow. However, they have a separate perspective, construction and style. Likely Dylan wrote them with some time in-between after putting down thoughts they developed from in his notebook.

The published lyrics do not correspond to the recording on *The Bootleg Series*

---

152 / Rodgers, Richard and Hammerstein II, Oscar, *The King and I*, 1951

Vol. 1-3. The fire and flame in line 3 are reversed; line 9 is "Tell me quick with a glance or a sigh;" line 13 and 14 on the record are "Is that the heat and the beat of your pulse that I feel/If it's not that what are you trying to conceal;"? line 21 asks "Are those rock and roll dreams in your eyes?"[153] Alternately, it's "do those neon lights blind your eyes;". Line 27 and 28 ask, "Is this some kind of game that you're playing with my heart/How deep must I go, where do I start?" Additionally, some minor word changes appear in the final verse, including a change to "anybody someone prays for."

Recording

April 21 was 'Tell Me' day at The Power Station. Six complete takes were put to tape, yielding two to choose for the compiled master reel. None of them line up in total with the published lyrics or the version released on *The Bootleg Series Vol. 1-3*.

The musicians rehearsed several treatments, while Dylan worked on lyrics and Knopfler co-ordinated with the engineers. The run tape reveals lyrics that appear only once, "Ever have the right kind of luck," "Do you have any weapons hidden back there in the dark" and "What you have in mind/what am I likely to find?" One very rough take makes it on to the session reel and includes the lyrics asking about being someone's plaything or toy or being like a waitress. As they practice and try to settle on a key, Knopfler tells Dylan he can just call out "middle 8" and it will be cut out later. Knopfler's fills are lovely in a moderate swing tempo. As they work, Dylan picks out lyrics from different drafts. Taylor plays a bit of 'Under the Boardwalk' as Dylan and Knopfler sort out the tempo, key and bridge. Knopfler is consistently encouraging and positive.

Forty minutes into the day, they begin serious recording. A ragged one-minute take, precedes a nearly five-minute take. This one includes lyrics asking about being someone's plaything or toy and the waitress comparison. Then comes words not found in writing or on other recordings: "Do you think of yourself being on a mountain top/are you one of the pigs or are you Queen of the Hop?" Taylor adds in a lap guitar part.

Dylan then suggested it be tried in another key, but they continue in D. Dylan

---

153 / In most other takes it is "Do those neon lights blind your eyes?"

picks up his harp and Clark is now on the B3 organ and Dylan on a 12-string. The first few verses have accompaniment added gradually until all are playing by the final bridge. Lyrically, the second verse begins, "Are you going someplace not saying where/do you even care?" Line 17 is tried as, "Can you ever be more than a stranger to me?" Dylan then tries lines 35 and 36 in this spot. For the bridge, he goes with the plaything/waitress combination, but then follows with, "Do you ever long to ride on that old ship of Zion/What's better to you, a live dog or a dead lion?" The question about going broke or going against the experts is also tried in this spot.

The next full take has the full accompaniment from the beginning and is noted as having "master potential," although the vocal seems a bit more hesitant than the prior track.

The following rough mix of the next take on the archive copy has a noticeable additional vocal track, indicating that there is an overdub that can't be fully made out. In fact, the engineer's track sheet indicates at least four Dylan vocal tracks on the "Great" key of E recording. Whether this also has the same number of vocals which another mix might treat differently, is probable but not provable from the available materials. This take was pulled to cassette for Dylan to review at his leisure.[154]

The final take is marked "great." Dylan's guitar is overdubbed on May 18, and his vocal—the product of compilation—is marked as being done on May 21.

The E key version on the compiled master has the Full Force backing vocals added on May 18. According to Michael Krogsgaard, Dylan was not present that day, so his vocals, including those indicated as lines 31 and 32 in the published lyrics, as well as others on the released record, were put down at some point after the master track. Regrettably, the date cannot be pin pointed.

---

154 / At the end of the 'Tell Me' work, and after Dylan seems to have left, Knopfler plays some of 'Going Home(Theme From Local Hero)' with Clark. The day ends with Clark playing a minute of Gershwin

14:

Foot of Pride (Too Late)

Published Lyrics
Foot of Pride (Too Late)

1   Like the lion tears the flesh off of a man

2   So can a woman who passes herself off as a male

3   They sang "Danny Boy" at his funeral and the Lord's Prayer

4   Preacher talking 'bout Christ betrayed

5   It's like the earth just opened and swallowed him up

6   He reached too high, was thrown back to the ground

7   You know what they say about bein' nice to the right people on the way up

8   Sooner or later you gonna meet them comin' down

9   Well, there ain't no goin' back

10   When your foot of pride come down

11   Ain't no goin' back

12   Hear ya got a brother named James, don't forget faces or names

13   Sunken cheeks and his blood is mixed

14   He looked straight into the sun and said revenge is mine

15   But he drinks, and drinks can be fixed

16   Sing me one more song, about ya love me to the moon and the stranger

17   And your fall-by-the sword love affair with Errol Flynn

18   In these times of compassion when conformity's in fashion

19   Say one more stupid thing to me before the final nail is driven in.

20   Well, there ain't no goin' back

21   When your foot of pride come down

22   Ain't no goin' back

23   There's a retired businessman named Red

24   Cast down from heaven and he's out of his head

25   He feeds off of everyone that he can touch

26   He said he only deals in cash or sells tickets to a plane crash
27   He's not somebody that you play around with much
28   Miss Delilah is his, a Phillistine is what she is
29   She'll do wondrous works with your fate, feed you coconut bread,
30   spice buns in your bed
31   If you don't mind sleepin' with your head face down in a grave

32   Well, there ain't no goin' back
33   When your foot of pride come down
34   Ain't no goin' back

35   Well, they'll choose a man for you to meet tonight
36   You'll play the fool and learn how to walk through doors
37   How to enter into the gates of paradise
38   No, how to carry a burden too heavy to be yours
39   Yeah, from the stage they'll be tryin' to get water outa rocks
40   A whore will pass the hat, collect a hundred grand and say thanks
41   They like to take all this money from sin, build big universities to study in
42   Sing 'Amazing Grace' all the way to the Swiss banks

43   Well, there ain't no goin' back
44   When your foot of pride come down
45   Ain't no goin' back

46   They got some beautiful people out there, man
47   They can be a terror to your mind and show you how to hold your
       tongue
48   They got mystery written all over their forehead
49   They kill babies in the crib and say only the good die young
50   They don't believe in mercy
51   Judgement on them is something that you'll never see
52   They can exalt you up or bring you down main route
53   Turn you into anything that they want you to be

54   Well, there ain't no goin' back

55   When your foot of pride come down

56   Ain't no goin' back

57   Yes, I guess I loved him too

58   I can still see him in my mind climbin' that hill

59   Did he make it to the top, well he probably did and dropped

60   Struck down by the strength of the will

61   Ain't nothin' left here partner, just the dust of a plague

62   that has left this whole town afraid

63   From now on, this'll be where you're from

64   Let the dead bury the dead. Your time will come

65   Let hot iron blow as he raised the shade

66   Well, there ain't no goin' back

67   When your foot of pride come down

68   Ain't no goin' back

Writing

Well, now we get to it, the Heart of the Matter (choose either Graham Greene or Don Henley), and what really kicked off my *Infidels* fascination nearly 40 years ago. Without the dense, weird, driving, hectoring 'Foot of Pride', it's unlikely I would have stayed on the trail until now. Without the stunning manner in which a (at first) truncated outtake hammered me from the start, it's likely I would have enjoyed it, put it away and pulled it out from time to time. Oh, no. It was a mystery that demanded to be investigated. What was it all about? Where does something like this come from? And, even more than '"Blind Willie McTell', how does it get shunted aside and left off the album?

The song is barely linear. There is an opening event and a closing foretelling of doom. An almost hazy evil pervades each of the verses. It could be what follows the birth of the prince in 'Jokerman.'

There are six verses, but many different drafts make it a total nearly 96 verses. None of them are in the spirit of 'Oh Happy Day'. If it is not a vision of Hell on Earth, it's a contender.

Before there was any information other than the recording itself (a complete version circulated a few months after a recording that cut off in line 46), someone (ahem) wrote an article in 1985.[155] The article, focused on the recording's lyrics being filled with images and scenes out of the *Book of Revelations* and was, while sincere, limited by what the author (ahem) did not know. The article was humble (as opposed to pedantic), well thought out, brilliantly written and ultimately full of crap, because what there was for us to hear from that time until now, was a song, but not the song. It was simply where Dylan stopped after months of conception, birth, shaping and reimagining.

We did know in 1985 that Dylan had worked hard on 'Foot of Pride', but not exactly how hard. In his early 1990s session history series in The Telegraph, Michael Krogsgaard identified 43 studio takes. There are 4 additional complete versions when we add in stunning versions on the run tape but are not on multitrack. The now more than 47 included incomplete, false starts and the like based on what engineers wrote down.

The Bob Dylan Archive® in Tulsa, Oklahoma provides insight into the volume of writing Dylan did on this song. There are 16 written drafts of the song that began as 'Too Late',[156]. A few differ by only a few words or lines, but the differences are significant. There are also thoughts on lyric pages for other songs which ultimately are incorporated into one of the developing "Foot/Too Late" drafts. One example is on a draft of 'Clean-Cut Kid', where Dylan wrote in capital letters: "MYSTERY BABYLON MOTHER OF WHORES." It has no connection with anything else on the page, so it seems Dylan was making a reminder for himself. And, it is one lone undeniable connection to *The Book of Revelations*.

Dylan's thought process, which could have begun months or years earlier, is first evidenced on the fourth page of the notebooks. Dylan wrote, "All I know is.... About the murder – he got dead let's just say that he been pushed." What appear to be very early drafts of the song start with "About the murder, I don't know."[157]

155 / Gans, Terry A. "It Was Like A Revelation—Bob Dylan's 'Foot of Pride'," *The Telegraph*, London Autumn 1985: 77-82

156 / The 'Foot of Pride' lyric does not appear until April 25th, the third day of recording the song, after 27 tries as 'Too Late'

Corruption is referred to in Notebook One as a "rotten tree" while "love carries an axe." Both concepts are included in one early recorded version of the song. 'Esther Brown' and a man who has "already ripped you off" and a "burden too heavy to bear" went from notebook to draft to studio.

By page 24 of his notebook, Dylan was experimenting with two different opening lines, which he would continue trying in the studio in April. One reflected on the murder, the other commented on "tears streaming down everybody's face." He also advanced to the framework on the second verse. In the lyrics, the brother has no name, but is "loved" and is "tall and thin" and only enters fights he can win. This was followed by thoughts that are later fixed to the opening about the narrator's disbelief about what the murder victim was accused of "because it wasn't his style."

That is the end of Dylan working on 'Foot of Pride' in his notebook. The next page shows him working on a song called 'While Men Die of Hunger', which is followed by parts of 'I & I'. At this point, the songwriting for 'Foot of Pride' progressed from notebook thoughts to written and typed drafts. Since *Water Pearl's* Captain Chris Bowman does not recall Dylan having a typewriter with him on board, true composing might have waited until on dry land.

In the archives, the lyrics for 'Foot of Pride/Too Late' are confusingly located in three different boxes, Numbers 35, 36 and 81. This could have been caused by an error in identification at the time the material was first curated years prior to its ultimate disposition to Tulsa.

Dylan wrote numerous lyrics for each of the verses. In the recording sessions, he chose and assembled from disparate drafts and often came up with spontaneous lyrics that matched no writing that was preserved. This synthesis created whole new versions of the song. There are common elements, however. The song drafts almost all begin with a death, sometimes a murder, sometimes a possible suicide or a death mourned at a funeral.

Each verse is followed by a chorus of "It's too late (X4).....to bring him back."

Who the "him" refers to or to where he might be brought is totally unclear, an example of what Joan Baez called Dylan's vagueness.

The second verse evolved serially from introducing "Mr. Blue" to "a good-looking guy with ice in his eye" to "a sharp looking guy with his mother's eyes," all of whom are facing some kind of unseen danger: "I'd say, "Look out Joe, it's a dirty stinking hole," or "Look out Joe, there's a fire below." Each of them drinks, and their drinks can be either drugged or fixed. The drafts read as if Dylan was just letting the thoughts and rhymes flow. Characters appear and depart: Mr. Penicillin, Miss Ann (a refugee), Miss Antoinette, a "man from Baltimore/seen it all before." So, in all versions, the second verse introduced a character until Dylan decided to settle on it being a brother: a "brother named Ace with an expressionless face" and a "brother from the tombs...a man of many unlit rooms." The evolution of this person continued throughout the recording process. Miss Ann, however, vanished.

The third verse revolved around a deceiver, identified as "the man upstairs with nine green eyes," later, a "retired businessman," then, a "retired businessman named Red." Red seeks to impose and control while giving "money to the church & foundations for research." These last eight words give a sense of the quick rhyming schemes Dylan attempted throughout his drafting. The manipulative Red is allied with a woman helper: Mary St. Clair, Mary Christine, Miss Brazil, Miss Not So Sweet, Hattie Belle and, ultimately, Delilah in the official lyrics. All these temptresses feed their target, some for a price, as long as he doesn't "mind sleeping with your head face down in the plate."

The fourth verse describes a man "you're" going to meet who is either going to tell you things you need to know, want to know or don't really want to know. Though you might like to learn "how to get rich quick," that probably would not be the case. It may explain how "you're" being manipulated or "how to commit slow suicide and not let it show." Distracting things are happening on stage, "the bumps and the grinds."

This verse parodies some televised evangelists and mentions a "whore" gathering funds from the followers, money that is spirited away to "secret rooms to count it up in" or Swiss banks by the final lyrics. In earlier drafts, all this razzle dazzle for the suckers, including book burning, leads not to salvation but to disillusion, such as losing one's wife all in pursuit of a non-existent "fairyland" or *Alice in Wonderland*.

The fifth verse maintains the "serious people" in almost every draft. They "don't come to party" and know how to "ring your bell and show you where the meat is hung." What appears as the final written draft brought back "mystery," the sole connection thus far to Revelations: "And upon her forehead was a name written, Mystery, Babylon the Great, the mother of harlots and abominations of the earth."[158] The last two lines of the fifth verse challenged Dylan until recording. He tried an image of serious people making "demons run and hide, they can take you for a ride." Nope, that was not it. How about putting your face on a postage stamp and "turn your home into an armed camp?" While not a keeper at the end, that was the line that was in the song through four days of recording.

In the sixth verse, the words "I loved him too" were in most drafts, as was the vision of the hill being climbed. In the written drafts, word and rhythmic play is maintained: "or was it wall, I don't recall, maybe it was a waterfall." Some versions have it as "another hole to fill;" some have "he didn't have time to leave a will" and a seeming filler "it doesn't matter and it never will." Dylan arrived at the "dust of fools" and the "dust of a plague," but it's hard to identify any written draft as final. There were various combinations for the final lines, including a "Doctor Bad, going back in a box to Trinidad." No more "social obligations" or "tears to shed" are what remained. One draft does include line 63 and the first half on line 64. But clearly, after so much writing, so many words, so many revisions, this was essentially an unfinished companion to 'Jokerman' when recording began on April 22.

None of the written verses contain the official (and recorded) first verse. As certain as we can be on anything, it was written after the April 27 session ended and before the April 29 session began.

The challenge for Dylan was to complete the song. In his mind, he may never have.

Recording

The first recording date, dedicated to what was initially titled 'Too Late', comes across as exploratory, a "let's see what we've got and what we've got to work on" exercise. The first run tape from April 22 began with early work on the melody and beat. Knopfler wanted a "short decay" on guitar "so it rings like chimes." He then counted in and led the band through several bars

158 / Book of Revelations, 17:5

to test the sound. In the background, Dylan faintly sang some lyrics. With little pause, the first full take was recorded on the session multitrack. The first few words are not decipherable but were followed by "I never believed it for a moment 'cause it wasn't his style." The victim was seen as a "threat to society" and was incongruously described as having "no bullets found in his chest, no needle marks on his arms." In later attempts the bullets jumped from none to 100. The brother in the second verse was one loved "with the spirit of a wild dove." A hug was the greeting, which forced the drinks being drugged rhyme. The description of "tall and thin, never fights a battle he can't win" made their only appearance in this take. The notebook jottings about love carrying an axe and rotten trees also survive for this initial version. The "final nail...in," from line 19, the only words from the published last four verse lines, was the single brick around which the eventual half-verse was built. In the third verse, the man with green eyes had disappeared, with retired businessman Red in place. His misdeed: "already ripped you off, but you are unaware." The bouncy rhyme of "money to the church/foundations for research" indicated one composition direction Dylan was trying. Red was not scared easily. The lines that followed were mumbled until "head face down in the plate."

The fourth verse, with the arranged meeting, continued with a playful delivery of what would be shown by "the man:" "How to get rich quick? Nah. I don't think so." Similar contradictions were in the final verse about what was being climbed—a hill, a wall, maybe a waterfall." At another day's session "was it this, was it that" was tried out in the opening verse. The trial and error—or the skill at composition—evident in the written versions go at full speed ahead in the studio. This verse, like all until the final day's recording, had bumps and grinds performed on the stage.[159] Lines 40-42 were locked in the song already.

In verse five, the "serious people" practiced infanticide and offered the cliché "only the good die young." Lines 50 and 51 were in this initial take, followed by the postage stamp/armed camp lines.

The final verse was pretty much the as published from line 61 on.

---

159 / Not to make too big a deal about it, many versions of 'Jokerman' have a stripper reference. 'St. James Infirmary Blues' was played in languid fashion in burlesque halls

This was an outstanding first take, one that with a few punch-ins could have been chosen for the album.

However, it wasn't the story the singer-songwriter wanted to tell or the way he wanted to present it. Dylan commented that Mick's part was "great, man," but that the take was too fast, "a little frantic for the tune." Knopfler said the sound of the organ was too thin.

Another take quickly broke down and Dylan complained that there were too many chords. After more rehearsing, mainly aimed at getting a comfortable tempo for the many words, Knopfler asked Dylan, "How does it feel, man? Do you want to try one like that?" Dylan responded, "I don't know." Knopfler: "Does it excite you so much you have to sit down?"

Dylan: "I don't know. I'm not sure if it's right for the tune." Dylan briefly preferred a beat similar to 'Someone's Got A Hold of My Heart' and in the next run-through even substituted some of that song's words, "You're the one I've been looking for," in line 16. This try broke down after the third verse, and Bob said, "there's something confusing in there."

On the next take, the group played two instrumental verses before Dylan came in.

He cut off and stated, "It's got to be so simple for this story to be told." Knopfler decided to get a 12-string, and Dylan took the time to sing a bit of 'Angel Flying Too Close To The Ground'.

Knopfler determinedly played the song on which they were supposed to be working on the 12-string, and Dylan's reaction was, "That's pretty, but it's still more of a percussion type rhythm," and sang "We Three." Knopfler did not know the chords so Dylan showed him and did the song again all the way through, even yodeling a bit on the word "eternity."

As they once more focused on 'Too Late', Dylan suggested a beat reminiscent of the Beatles' 'Get Back'. The guitar sound was raw and a driving bass line stepped down at the chorus. Dylan really sang it here, vocally rough and removed from the sweetness in the prior takes and spontaneously threw in some new lyrics. Taylor was given space for an energetic solo. While the engineers noted, "good feel," the power and vocal style of this attempt was not pursued further this day. However, the recording was pulled for Bob's cassette, and the overall vocal sound was reflected in the final take a week later. It's an intriguing treatment, but for one of the few times in the sessions Knopfler seemed slightly irked. A reel switch probably coincided with a break for the participants.

The tape that is labeled "Run #1" is actually the second tape from April 22 and is not continuous. On it, Dylan played Buddy Holly's 'Heartbeat',[160] Christmas songs and other covers (Chapter 22). For 30 minutes, there was little recorded on the tape resembling the chords or rhythm of "Too Late." When they returned to the song, they worked on the beginning with the first chorus and Dylan experimented with choices from his wide assortment of available lyrics. He said, "That's kind of the general idea," and immediately proceeded into a mostly instrumental of 'If I Give My Heart To You', written by Jimmy Brewster, Jimmie Crane and Al Jacobs. It was a number four hit for Doris Day in 1954.[161]

Work on 'Too Late' for April 22 concluded with a five minute 'Reggae Jam', conceivably a Knopfler experiment. Afterward, Dylan started in on Christmas songs, which in no way could seriously be considered work for a seasonal album. He jokingly said after one, "There's two songs for a Christmas album." But he was playing around, just as when he launched into 'Cha Cha' (or 'Choo Choo) Boogie' and asked for synthesizer accompaniment. He was notably saving further work on 'Foot of Pride/Too Late' for another day.

The day concluded with a near-falsetto 'Silent Night in E'. Dylan was quite taken with the sounds coming from the synth. Then comes a verse of 'Oh Come All Ye Faithful', 'Lover's Concerto' and 'Dark as a Dungeon'. "Old Merle, Travis He'll like it. I don't know if he'll like it, (But) if it don't sell records, he won't like it," Dylan commented.

What good is having a studio and top musicians to play with if you can't have yourself a little fun?

The next day, April 23, was all for 'Too Late' and the last day before the

---

160 / The only other time Dylan is known to have played 'Heartbeat' was in Philadelphia November 23, 2014. It was in an afternoon concert for one person, Fredrik Wikingsson. Wikingsson took part in a Swedish television program *Experiment Ensam (Experiment Alone)*

161 / Eight years later in his interview with *SongTalk's* Paul Zollo, Dylan questioned the sentimentality of and motivation behind such songs: "'If I Give My Heart To You,' who gives a shit?"
Unedited recording of the interview which appeared on *Singers and Songwriters*.
Paul Zollo and Louise Goffin, The Great Song Adventure, PodcastApril 15 2019

Bob Dylan, Los Angeles, October 1983. Photo: Aaron Rapoport/Corbis/Getty Images.

Top left: Mark Robinson and Dylan at 'Sweetheart Like You' video shoot. Courtesy Mark Robinson. Left: Chris Bowman, skipper and builder of 'Dylan's yacht', Water Pearl. Above: The Water Pearl off Anguilla. Photo: Guy N Harris/Getty Images. Right: The author in the archive with the notebooks. Far right: Sly Dunbar and Robbie Shakespeare (present day).

Bob Dylan, New York,
February 1983.
Photo by Lynn Goldsmith/
Corbis/VCG via Getty Images.

Bob Dylan and Mick Taylor June 19, 1984. Photo by Rob Verhorst/Redferns.

Bob Dylan and Mark Knopfler in the Power Station studio. Courtesy The Bob Dylan Archive®/Albert and David Maysles.

Studio A, The Power Station, New York.

Top: Bob Dylan and Dinah Shore talk Chevy, March 15, 1982, Songwriters Hall of Fame. Photo by Lynn Goldsmith/Corbis/VCG via Getty Images.
Above: In the studio with Josh Abbey (far left) and Joe Walsh(middle) 1988. Courtesy Josh Abbey.

Right: Infide[l]
producer, Mark Knopf[t]
and his manag[er]
Ed Bicknell. Courte[sy]
Ed Bickne[ll]

*Above: Clinton Heylin (left)
shares a rare opinion with
Terry Gans, October 2018.
Photo: Mark Davidson at
The Bob Dylan Archive®. Far
left: Bob Dylan, Rick Danko,
Levon Helm, Lone Star Café,
February 16, 1983. Photo
by Lynn Goldsmith/Corbis/
VCG via Getty Images. Left:
Tape box from the Infidel's
sessions. Right: Engineer
Neil Dorfsman and Producer
Mark Knopfler.*

Bob Dylan, Los Angeles, October 1983. Photo by Aaron Rapoport/ Corbis/Getty Images.

song became 'Foot of Pride'.[162] The run tapes recorded much more than the session reels and document that Knopfler wanted to try the song with acoustic accompaniment. Before they began, Knopfler cautioned that there would be leakage from the guitar. Dylan sang two verses, and then Knopfler said, "Let me try it this way, with a pick." "Okay," Bob playfully said, "Don't let my guitar leak now," then warbled a few lines of 'Over the Rainbow'. Knopfler then played an acoustic backing for Bob to sing 'Too Late' "but sensed Dylan's unease. "No?" Knopfler asked. "No, not really," Bob responded. "It's nice. I'm just not used to it that way. You know I can already hear it."

Dylan unsuccessfully tried to demonstrate on his guitar how he heard it. Bob said, "I think it's my fault." Knopfler said, "It's your fault for writing it." A wonderfully sung acoustic version followed this exchange. It's a revelation to hear since none of us had heard anything other than the bootlegged and then the released version for reference since 1983.

Dylan had clearly worked on rewriting lyrics overnight. He made some slight vocal stumbles on the final two lines, but overall delivered smooth singing and a strong harmonica part. The "being nice to the right people on the way up," the Errol Flynn romance, fashion/compassion combination and line 19 appeared for the first time.

In the third verse, businessman Red was replaced by Dr. Silver Spoon who "owns the Embassy Ballroom." Miss Esther Brown was now Miss Rosanna Black "from the other side of the track."

Verse four had the "man" offering to open some doors. The desire to learn "how to enter the gates of Paradise" was sung. Lines 50 and 51 were in place. "Maybe it was a wall, maybe it was a waterfall" were still a part of the wordplay in the final verse, but now the "hot iron" blows when "you raise the shade."

"Let's go back to the original way," Dylan requested. This "original" way is not

---

162 / *Psalms*, 36:11
The words "Let not the foot of pride some against me/upon me" are found in the writing of David's. There are numerous interpretations as to the meaning, but many agree the "foot" belonged to David's arrogant enemies, not pride in himself. He trusted the Lord to protect him. This verse is almost certainly where Dylan got the words, whether from leafing through a Bible on his off day or recovered from prior jottings

on any earlier recording. Dylan then decided, "Maybe we should just cut another song. Well, I'll have to come back late at night, with nobody here, when all the lights are low...This song? It doesn't have the simplest foundation to it. It's too complicated. The words, it's hard to throw them all out there like that...it's easy to throw them out there, but it's what's underneath it." Mark was positive, "We'll get it. No problem."

Dylan moved to the piano for a few minutes and then left the room. Knopfler listened to a playback of the complete take from ten minutes before. On Dylan's return, Knopfler and Shakespeare worked on some foundational 12-string and bass parts. Bob sang a verse to this beat with a more relaxed and less insistent vocal and finished with some Floyd Kramer piano flourishes. He was still searching for "something consistent in it." He sang a few verses from the top, and line 13 was "Where Miss Daisy plays and the reviews have been mixed."

After two lines of the third verse, Dylan asked, "What about that way?" Mark asked if Robbie is happy. "Yeah, mon," he responded. "Alright, let's do that," Dylan said and counted off.

The next take had a slightly punchier feel. Two women were at the scene of whatever happened, but were veiled, keeping the events a mystery, but now "he reached too high and tumbled back down to the ground." A plethora of "you knows" populate almost every line of the first verse.

The brother was now Paul who "hangs out at the Cafe Royale" and Miss Dolly plays to mixed reviews. Paul was "pretty to look at/looking for someone to throw the book at." "You knows" continued in this take seemingly unchecked. The woman was Miss Rosetta Blake who "lives on both sides of the lake." And coconut bread was now served along with spiced buns.

At the arranged meeting "you'll" find the key "to enter the Gates of Paradise... No, not really," Dylan sang. What was really learned was the ability to manage a burden not your own.

The "nothing left here partner" is described as "just the dust of fools and phantoms". An incomplete take marked "nice feel" opened with the old "about the murder" scenario. The narrator didn't recall because he was "playing a clarinet, no wait I was visiting a friend in jail." The veiled women were still no help.

After a couple of false starts, a take kicked off with "They say he died standing up," but the singer can't be certain because he still was either playing the clarinet or on a jail visit.

Brother Paul and Dr. Silver Spoon continued in their roles, but the Doctor now "feeds off everyone he can touch."

Dylan decided, "There's something too hectic" and cut off the take. Knopfler vowed, "We're going to get it because we're not going to leave here." Bob speculated that perhaps he was doing the vocal wrong and perhaps should sing through a vocoder.[163] Dylan once more left the room as Mark said "Don't give up on it, Bob," who replied he was just going to look for his t-shirt. When Dylan returned, he suggested some organ changes to Clark.

Ten minutes later, with the lights lowered at Dylan's request, the musicians complete a take with pretty much the same tempo, noted as "Rockin'" on the engineer's sheet, which also said "best tempo." Dylan roughened his delivery and extended the final word of each verse with a passionate delivery. It was marked as Knopfler and Taylor's favorite.

In this version, the two women didn't "see a thing" because "both of them were wearing masks, no wait they were wearing veils."

Esther Black returned, and now she lived on both sides of the lake.

A spirited minute-plus harp break came between the third and fourth verse, a clue to Dylan's investment in this take. The money from sin was used to build "big castles to study in."

The "Serious People" were still ringing "your bell," but now they showed you "how to hold your tongue," rather than where the "meat is hung."

Another strong harp solo played out the nearly nine-minute take.

During the ensuing break, Dylan jammed with a piano-driven bluesy way to sing the song. He followed this with a blues riff about "92nd Street....a dog in heat...people treat you like a thief." Then, verses of "Lord Protect My Child" were sung off-mic as Dylan strummed.

Dylan liked a picking style Knopfler was playing and practiced to it several times. At one point he tried a G minor chord to accompany "meet them coming down."

As they started a new take Dylan requested, "Can I have some more pain in my

---

163 / A voice modification device with a synthesizer between the vocal mic and the recording tape

ear?" The performance is a little rushed, marring a strong vocal and harp part. The recording sheet noted, "Bob, no." Another take was at a slightly faster pace and Bob was pleased, "That's it. That's the right way." Mark said, "Let's keep that one as a reference and do it properly tomorrow." Bob concurred, "That's the way... we should keep that one." At the end, Robbie said, "Mark, this is reggae we're playing in now. Lots of different kinds of rhythm."

Ironically, at the end of the take when Bob said, "that's it," and work ended for Saturday April 23, it became too late for 'Too Late.' After a Sunday tampering with the song, as he told Paul Zollo he was prone to do with *Infidels*, there was a new song title[164] and some new styles.

As they began work on April 25, the melody and beat resembled a Native American chant stood on its head. An electric piano and an abbreviated wah-wah effect on guitar, which Dylan called an underwater sound, added to the overall weirdness of what was a rehearsal take.

Dylan had crafted a new beginning, including the earth-swallowing image. There was a "bad wife" who wanted her husband drunk.

And there was a new chorus:

"There ain't no going back, ain't no going back, when that foot of pride comes down ain't no going back." Knopfler contributed a chuck-a-luck rhythm underneath, and Taylor's fills were somewhat understated. Once more, Dylan's lyrics had the narrator not there for the opening events. Now, though, we had a funeral singing of 'Danny Boy'[165] and 'The Lord's Prayer'. Because the singer was still visiting a jail, he had the preacher referring to Christ's "betrayal." Lines 7 and 8 were now in place. Paul remained at the Cafe, and Miss Pixie played to mixed reviews. Paul was on the borderline, a rhyme for "revenge is mine." The requested "one more song" was about "whiskey heaven."

Red was now hanging out at the Motorside ballroom, "where slave trade blooms," infecting all he touched. The Gates of Paradise were "bloody."

The serious people were now in "an invisible world." They "can turn you into the devil's daughter, lead you into the valley of slaughter." And, if you're subjected to them, they will have you believing you haven't changed.

---

164 / The recording sheets would continue to use the original title until April 29
165 / In some communities, it is de rigueur for 'Danny Boy' to be part of a funeral

It was a complete take, although the engineer's sheet had a question mark about it. In the next two-and-a-half-minute try, Miss Trixie was now at the Cafe.

The next complete take was rightly marked as "too slow," but Dylan was getting comfortable with the vocal delivery required by the beat. He did have trouble, as he seemed to have had almost from the start, with describing the interchangeable character that at this moment was Miss Rosetta Black. There were simply too many words for one line: "been to both sides of the lake, she's rough to look at but she's straight."

A new reel began with essentially the same musical treatment, just about as slow as its predecessor. The pounding bass, the guitar accents and the electric piano were kept. The Rosetta Black line was still problematic. Now she had been "to the bottom of the lake and back," but again Dylan could not sing the words without stumbling.

The chorus was delivered five times after the final verse to drive home the point that there "ain't no going back."

There were a couple of minutes of a try at a smoother vocal that sounds reminiscent of 'Someone's Got a Hold of My Heart'. Indeed, that song then interrupted work on 'Foot of Pride' for four incomplete or false starts, followed by a complete take, all of which is discussed in Chapter Ten.

After enjoying the equivalent of a palate cleanser by way of 'Someone', it was back to work on 'Foot of Pride'. The brother was now "James who could walk through the flames...puts his cash on the line." At the Ballroom, there were the 'slave-trade blues.' The beautiful people "lead you like a lamb to slaughter." The team gave it five more tries, two complete, to close April 25. But God love them, the next day they kept trying.

As the band and Dylan worked through the late attempts, the wife in the song was "an unrighteous woman who could have passed herself as a male," an image Dylan refined until the final version. The first appearance of mixed-blood brother James came in the first of the two complete takes. Red was in the Ecstasy Ballroom but now was described as feeding off "everyone he can touch." Knopfler and Shakespeare put down a hard, steady backbone for the number while Taylor riffed on lead.

The day's final take was marked "best yet" and pulled to cassette for Dylan. The first two verses saw some hesitations and stumbles in Dylan's delivery, but the take was cited as the "best yet. " This may have been due to the accompaniment. Someone in a later archival document noted "Eddie Cochran" to describe the sound. Once he got by the first two verses, Dylan's delivery is strong.

As the festivities began the next day, the musicians played two minutes of instrumentals of the first two verses and chorus. Sly and Alan wanted to hear the vocal. Dylan said, "You didn't get the vocal? Play the vocal back for him." Alan caught on and called it a "silent vocal, never been done before." Dylan then said, "We've got to do this song, it's going to become..." Unfortunately, the word he said next was drowned out by an otherworldly synth sound and some stray notes until Knopfler cracked the whip and counted in for the first in a series of instrumental workups.

Twenty minutes into the session, before they began again, Dylan had pleaded, "Just got to get through it one time. That's all that counts." The first line was new: "Just like the lion tears to flesh off a man." It was linked to "a woman" rather than the unrighteous wife. The rewrite of James remembering faces and names was in place. James' sunken cheeks were described as well (lines 12-13). No more Ecstasy Ballroom for Red. The final third verse was delivered in its entirety. In verse four, the stage was now free from bumps and the grinds, which gave way to an attempt to get water from rocks. The money from sin, collected by a "great whore," was given "to people with the right-color skin." The "mystery written all over their foreheads" line entered the song. The wonderful "They can exalt you up or bring you down bankrupt" line had been added. This take broke down before the last verse.

Clark expressed himself and others agreed it was too slow. "Too slow," Bob finally responded, "Tell me one thing that's not too slow. Hockey? I don't know what's too slow about it. I could be slower, could be faster, too. Hey Neil, we could do it a little faster, the way Roy Orbison would do it, or Debby Boone."

Dylan and crew did make it through the last take of the day for 'Foot of Pride', but the delivery was not smooth. The accompaniment was also somewhat sluggish. With the sin money, "They go to secret places to divide it up in." Dylan sang the chorus three times at the end.

The lyrics were essentially complete and the story was a long way from the drafts and recordings of the first couple of days. Now, if they could only get the music and vocal to Dylan's satisfaction...

These attempts restarted on April 27 after something identified simply as "From Paul." (No clue!)

Dylan needed a couple of false starts to get ready to sing and then tried to remember how he sang it the night before. In the first of two complete takes, Dylan had access to so many words from months of working on the song that there were continued stumbles.

Dylan called for another take and delivered a more rapid-fire vocal. He made only a couple of very minor lyrical variations, such as the people in line 47 could "divide your mind." It was perfectly good take, but Dylan was waist-deep into trying to get some result known only to himself and pushed on two days later for a final time.

April 29th was the last hurrah for 'Foot of Pride'. It was make-or-break time. After filling two digital reels with various jams, noodling, improvised songs, chestnuts like 'Buttons and Bows' and 'Home on the Range', Dylan and company got down to the "Foot." An instrumental run-through started off, followed by one false start. The first full take was closer to what was released in 1991 on *The Bootleg Series Vol. 1-3*. The tempo and harmonica fills showed the way toward the keeper. Up until the final take, the song this day opened with "Like the lion." Dylan reverted to "whisky drinking angel" instead of "love me 'til the morning stranger," and that seemed to throw him for the following few lines. The sheets indicate that this take included "original organ and bass," and was pulled for Bob's cassette.

Dylan tried a series of eight vocal delivery tests, including a Leslie effect swirling organ lead-in that hearkens back to early versions of 'Blind Willie McTell'. Engineer Josh Abbey guesses two Leslie speakers were spinning (one on the overdubbed B3) at different speeds, probably a one-time idea someone wanted to try.[166] Only one organ is on the released mix. The archives version is the product of multiple mixes of the same multitrack tape that was the master used for *The Bootleg Series Vol. 1-3*. At midpoint through these short attempts, Dylan said, "I'm sorry, I'm sorry" about all these fits and starts. But the following minute-and-a-half still showed the accompaniment was not quite together. "I think this is the toughest song I've tried to do in my entire recording career,"

166 / Josh Abbey, email April 27, 2019

Dylan confessed. "I've never struggled with any song like this one."

A nearly four-minute take featured harder and deeper drums. When the track broke down at 3:37, Dylan's frustration was obvious: "Why don't you just keep playing it?" he asked one of the musicians.

After a short false-start, he then he proceeded directly into what would become the belatedly released (although speedily bootlegged) version. The recording sheets indicate "New B3 and bass," and two organs are evident in the final two choruses.

This was easily Dylan's best delivery of the vocals and, with no indication of any later work on this song until December 1990, the run tape shows it was a live take. It was a tour de force. "This is it" the tape sheet proclaims, but "it" was not written by anyone at that time. Dylan seemed to agree, "Except there was one wrong change, but who cares at this point?"

This was the track that might have felt like forever in coming to those involved. The lyrics had solidified to the point where there was a unity between the "reached too high and fell back to the ground" of the first verse and the "did he make it to the top, well he probably did and dropped" of the last verse.

Despite all this work, 'Foot of Pride' apparently was not considered for the album. One reason put forth long ago by "The Dylan Camp" was that the bass sped up. Hundreds of listening by my admittedly untrained ears have not picked that up, certainly not in any way to make an appreciable difference.

Dylan has said in interviews that if a song "hangs around too long," he loses interest. The result of 'Foot of Pride' is certainly far from its origins as 'Too Late'. Great as someone who writes 6,700 words about the song might think that it is, it could be that its author simply considered it unfinished and the story still not told. This toughest song was never resolved.

15:

Union Sundown

Published Lyrics
Union Sundown

1	Well, my shoes, they come from Singapore
2	My flashlight's from Taiwan
3	My tablecloth's from Malaysia
4	My belt buckle's from the Amazon
5	You know, this shirt I wear comes from the Philippines
6	And the car I drive is a Chevrolet
7	It was put together down in Argentina
8	By a guy makin' thirty cents a day
9	Well, it's sundown on the union
10	And what's made in the U.S.A.
11	Sure was a good idea
12	Til greed got in the way
13	Well, this silk dress is from Hong Kong
14	And the pearls are from Japan
15	Well, the dog collar's from India
16	And the flower pot's from Pakistan
17	All the furniture, it says "Made in Brazil"
18	Where a woman, she slaved for sure
19	Bringin' home thirty cents a day to a family of twelve
20	You know, that's a lot of money to her
21	Well, it's sundown on the union
22	And what's made in the U.S.A.
23	Sure was a good idea
24	'Til greed got in the way
25	Well, you know, lots of people complainin' that there is no work
26	I say, "Why you say that for

27 When nothin' you got is U.S.–made?"
28 They don't make nothin' here no more
29 You know, capitalism is above the law
30 It say, "It don't count 'less it sells"
31 When it costs too much to build it at home
32 You just build it cheaper someplace else

33 Well, it's sundown on the union
34 And what's made in the U.S.A.
35 Sure was a good idea
36 'Til greed got in the way

37 Well, the job that you used to have
38 They gave it to somebody down in El Salvador
39 The unions are big business, friend
40 And they're goin' out like a dinosaur
41 They used to grow food in Kansas
42 Now they want to grow it on the moon and eat it raw
43 I can see the day coming when even your home garden
44 Is gonna be against the law

45 Well, it's sundown on the union
46 And what's made in the U.S.A.
47 Sure was a good idea
48 'Til greed got in the way

49 Democracy don't rule the world
50 You'd better get that in your head
51 This world is ruled by violence
52 But I guess that's better left unsaid
53 From Broadway to the Milky Way
54 That's a lot of territory indeed
55 And a man's gonna do what he has to do
56 When he's got a hungry mouth to feed

57   Well, it's sundown on the union
58   And what's made in the U.S.A.
59   Sure was a good idea
60   'Til greed got in the way

Writing

Is Dylan writing about The Union—the United States—or labor unions? It could be both, although he specifically mentions "the unions," and the song covers how manufacturing that used to be done in America is now being done abroad. The song is a commentary on an economic reality and resultant social disruption. The central lines, which place it firmly with the spirit of *Infidels*, are lines 49 through 51: "Democracy don't rule the world/You'd better get that in your head/This world is ruled by violence."

No part of the song appears in the notebooks. There is a line about "dirty mouths to feed" which could reflect the later line 56, but it's a stretch to connect them.

Three draft legal pads are pages in the archives.[167] Dylan mused that when profits are down for manufacturers, they are going to have to go on food relief. He listed different items: tablecloth, belt buckle, rope, neck tie, high chair, pearls. Then he listed the various countries where the items could be produced more cheaply than in the U.S. He pointed out the irony of people who sought the lowest price and then lamented the lack of work in America. Capitalism followed its own laws in only producing what can be sold, he noted. "Somebody got to take control," he said, "nobody seems up to the task."

Dylan was prescient in a number of areas, although he had visited the impacts of moving American mining jobs offshore 20 years previously in 'North Country Blues'.[168] His remark about "even your home garden's gonna be against the law" was not a throwaway. In the Florida 2019 legislative session, bills came out of the House and Senate to prohibit local jurisdictions from forbidding front-yard

167 / BDA, 2016.01 B36 F04 1, 2
168 / "They complained in the East They are paying too high
They say that your ore ain't worth digging That it's much cheaper down
In the South American towns
Where the miners work almost for nothing."
Bob Dylan, 'North Country Blues', *The Times They Are A-Changin'*, 1964

gardens. No vote was taken before the session ended.[169] In the May 5, 2019 *New York Times Magazine*, an article detailed the closing of four auto manufacturing plants in the United States, putting 14,000 out of work, and including a Chevrolet plant in Lordstown, Ohio. The wage differential with $2.60 an hour Mexican labor was seen as a rational Capitalist[170] Choice. The Unions, who had little clout in 2019 to protect their members, were already seen as "dinosaurs" by Dylan in 1983.

In one of those coincidence, perhaps not a coincidence situations, there is an exchange between two gangsters in Francois Truffaut's (which Dylan notes in the liner notes to his third album) *Shoot the Piano Player*: "Snorkel(pen) from America.... belt..from Oceana.....suit comes from London and it's made from Australian wool...shoes made of Egyptian leather."

Whether one considers the song a protest, a message or another observation of man inventing his doom, it was not a crackpot point of view,[171] as one reviewer claimed.

Recording

Dylan began recording 'Union Sundown' an hour into the April 27 session. That day also included initial work on "the newly titled 'Foot of Pride'," production of the master for 'I And I' and recording of the ultimately discarded 'Julius and Ethel'. In between, Dylan gave three runs at 'Union Sundown', a song he would complete at the penultimate *Infidels* session on May 2. His initial effort was essentially to get the chords and tempo down. Only the chorus had actual lyrics at this point. Dylan briefly strummed the bass strings of his guitar and sang by himself to reacquaint himself with the melody and meter. He fumbled around and said, "That's gonna be good," provoking laughter because it was not at that time. When he did capture the chords, the musicians quickly got into the spirit of the number. There are no recordings of earlier rehearsals but when Dylan simply said "Union" to Knopfler, Mark knew what to play. After a run-through, Dylan commented, "I don't have the lyrics for that." A five-minute work-up, again with

169 / Florida House of Representatives, 2019 Bills, HB145

170 / Latoya Ruby Frazier and Dan Kaufman, 'What Happens To a Factory Town When the Factory Shuts Down?' *New York Times Magazine*, May 5, 2019

171 / Robert Christgau, website

dummy lyrics but blistering accompaniment, was marked as "Bob's favorite," and after Dylan announced, "That's called 'Union Sundown', the take was retained for later work on May 2. Presumably, the interim was when writing on the legal pad produced the complete song. At the April 27 session, the only verse he had tried involved shoes which came from different locales.

The May 2 session saw the most reels of tape used—five—and probably was the most time consuming. Dylan devoted no fewer than 11 takes to Willie Nelson's 'Angel Flying Too Close To The Ground', seven to his own 'Lord, Protect My Child', three complete takes to 'Union Sundown', and two serious covers of 'Green Green Grass of Home'.

For 'Union Sundown', Dylan had now developed a complete set of lyrics. After he finished recording 'Lord Protect My Child', and heard some Knopfler country picking, Bob said, "Let's do that "Union" thing. What key was it in?" Mark answers "A." Dylan decided they should listen to the earlier recording to get the feel. A complete run-through was a rehearsal for the vocal. It was not without commitment but basically was an exercise to become comfortable with fitting the words to the accompaniment. Dylan liked the feel, "Let's try to do it like that." The lyrics deviated from official lyrics and the album There were lines regarding "religious capitalism, under corporate command...it says no one gets hired to do anything that can be done cheaper in another land." The published lines 29 through 32 are arguably a more refined way of saying the same thing. Dylan noted the "big profits" made by drug dealers, who could safely escape the consequences of the damage they produced. The original final verse, which would have extended the song by well over a minute, pictured the U.S. President (any President it seems) as a total figurehead who is to do what he is told by corporate bosses. The take is noted as "the one" and initially was marked as the master, until "Not" was written in.

The true final take in terms of Dylan plus the core band, included singer Clydie King[172] on the chorus and came after a break and 'Green Green Grass of Home'.

---

172 / Clydie Mae King began her professional career in the Fifties. Although she recorded as a lead singer, her reputation was made as a back-up singer for Ray Charles, The Rolling Stones, Linda Ronstadt and many others – including Bob Dylan in the first half of the Eighties. Often, she duetted with Dylan, who told *Rolling Stone* at her 2019 death "She was my ultimate singing partner. No one ever came close. We were two soulmates."

The lyrics on the final take of 'Union Sundown' in the archives are close to the released take, although there are some differences in the vocals. Evidence shows vocal overdubs recorded May 18, June 8 and test edits on June 10 and work followed on June 15. Dylan's vocal in the archives mix may not totally come from May 2. King's part is on the run tape, so hers was May 2. On the archive tape, the final official verse is included twice (It may be the exact same recording duplicated.), but the "man in the mask in the White House" is not. Dylan said he messed up, but" that's ok," and asked if it's still... Then the recording cut off.

The work on June 10 included "vocal fly ins," which is the process of moving digital information, instruments or vocals, from one area of the song to another. In this case, Dylan's chorus vocal was copied from the multitrack to a segment of two track tape. Then, engineers recorded what they had flown off back onto the multitrack for a different chorus. In the days before Pro Tools or sampling technology, it was the true technical magic that allowed for Dylan's ideas to be quickly executed.[173]

Those who may tend to skip over 'Union Sundown' because they don't like post-Sixties Dylan actually talking about societal issues miss out on Knopfler's persistent rhythm guitar, Taylor's slide, Clark's barroom piano and a committed (perhaps overly so) vocal from Dylan.

Dylan fit the song into concert setlists five times in 1986 and 24 times in 1992, most likely to have a driving rocker. In these performances, he paid far more attention to delivering the chorus than to the verses.

---

173 / Email, Josh Abbey May 8, 2019: "How we did this:
1) copy the chorus vocal to the 2-track. Mark the 2-track with a grease pencil where the 'flown off' piece begins
2) wind the 2-track backward by hand so you can still see your mark
3) run the multitrack from before the spot you want to insert the fly in. Punch into record on the track
4) start the 2-track at beats in the song (trial and error) while recording what's on the 2-track to the multitrack
5) repeat steps 3 and 4 until it sounds good. When it sounds right in its new home-job done"

CHAPTER 15 / UNION SUNDOWN

16:

I And I

Published Lyrics
I And I

1	Been so long since a strange woman has slept in my bed
2	Look how sweet she sleeps, how free must be her dreams
3	In another lifetime she must have owned the world, or been faithfully wed
4	To some righteous king who wrote psalms beside moonlit streams
5	I and I
6	In creation where one's nature neither honors nor forgives
7	I and I
8	One says to the other, no man sees my face and lives
9	Think I'll go out and go for a walk
10	Not much happenin' here, nothin' ever does
11	Besides, if she wakes up now, she'll just want me to talk
12	I got nothin' to say, 'specially about whatever was
13	I and I
14	In creation where one's nature neither honors nor forgives
15	I and I
16	One says to the other, no man sees my face and lives
17	Took an untrodden path once, where the swift don't win the race
18	It goes to the worthy, who can divide the word of truth
19	Took a stranger to teach me, to look into justice's beautiful face
20	And to see an eye for an eye and a tooth for a tooth
21	I and I
22	In creation where one's nature neither honors nor forgives
23	I and I
24	One says to the other, no man sees my face and lives

25   Outside of two men on a train platform there's nobody in sight

26   They're waiting for spring to come, smoking down the track

27   The world could come to an end tonight, but that's all right

28   She should still be there sleepin' when I get back

29   I and I

30   In creation where one's nature neither honors nor forgives

31   I and I

32   One says to the other, no man sees my face and lives

33   Noontime, and I'm still pushin' myself along the road, the darkest part

34   Into the narrow lanes, I can't stumble or stay put

35   Someone else is speakin' with my mouth, but I'm listening only to my heart

36   I've made shoes for everyone, even you, while I still go barefoot

37   I and I

38   In creation where one's nature neither honors nor forgives

39   I and I

40   One says to the other, no man sees my face and lives

Writing

Twenty-six pages into the first of his 1983 notebooks, Dylan wrote a line about a strange woman sleeping in his bed and how long a time it had been. It appeared to be the first writing of ideas that became 'I And I', the most obviously island-influenced of the *Infidels* album. An argument can be made that these pages of the notebook are Dylan's familiarizing himself with a song already partly written. This arises from the near completeness of the first verse, albeit with some differences from the final version. A woman's dreams are described as "hard." But this was followed by small notes about the sweetness of the sleep of "soft" dreams. The line about the other lifetime and the marriage to the psalm writing king were on the page.

Unfortunately, no typed draft lyrics—indeed any lyrics other than in the notebook or for pre- publication review—have been found in the archives.

CHAPTER 16 / I AND I

Partially written does not, of course, mean fully written. The protagonist's emotions were not completely driven by affection in some lines. Twice Dylan worked with the thought of being a stranger or visitor in his own house. Worse, the action accompanying these feelings is "whispering 'I Love You' to a deaf mute."

The two men on the train platform are either waiting for a ghost or Noah's Ark. The narrator goes out for a walk because he has a lot on his mind and he doesn't really want to sleep.

The final verse, which appeared after the vipers in the streets image from a note for 'Don't Fall Apart On Me Tonight', was virtually complete, lacking only the final two lines. He worked toward that end two notebook pages later and wrote the concluding lines at the bottom of the page.

Two pages later, Dylan wrote "I and I, walking through meadow land during the rain." Page 34, the last lyric work in this notebook that can be identified with any song, finalized lines 27 and 28.

The song follows a specific timeline: early to mid-evening; later at night; probably morning (seeing the men waiting for a train); noon. It's a wandering journey. The mood of the draft lyrics encompassed sleeplessness, dislocation and a desire to leave for a time. Competing with the restlessness is a fear that the night's partner won't understand he had not left for good. Similar feelings were expressed in draft lyrics for 'Someone's Got A Hold of My Heart' and early on in 'Don't Fall Apart on Me Tonight'. They were resolved in different fashions in each song. In 'Someone's Got A Hold Of My Heart', the partner was reassured that he's only, "Going to get my coat...Somewhere I got to be." In 'Don't Fall Apart On Me Tonight' the woman was invited to sit with the narrator, they ain't going anywhere. In 'I And I', he was banking on her "still be sleeping when I get back." The drafts hint at a *Rashomon*[174] look at the same scene through different eyes.

As noted in Chapter One, when Dylan spoke to Paul Zollo, he referred to 'I And I' as "one of them Caribbean songs."

The chorus and the title of the song are not directly tied to the verses. The chorus neither detracts from the mood or path of the song nor adds to it. It

---

174 / *Rashomon* is a classic 1950 Japanese movie which today is considered one of the greatest films of all time. It was filmed by the legendary Akira Kurosawa, and demonstrates how truth is skewed by perception and motive

simply complements the vague sense of dissatisfaction and mystery. The last lines reflect upon the gifts the narrator/writer bestowed upon others while he was left wanting.

What of the words "I And I?" As it is Jamaican, specifically Rastafarian, it defies precise translation. Many sources contend it is the equivalent of "I myself." Others say the concept is a person's physical body and mind are one with the soul. Another interprets it as "we." Still others may believe it an expression of the speaker's physical being in oneness with Jah, God. All human language is initially learned from parents or their equivalents. Use of "I And I" was part of the learned Jamaican language, and according to ship builder and captain Chris Bowman, his crew used the term all the time. What it meant to Dylan, beyond language for verse is anyone's guess.

Recording

April 27 was a session of different styles. Dylan was still busily searching for a rhythm and accompaniment for 'Foot of Pride' and redoing lyrics at the same time. He made a first pass at the driving rocker 'Union Sundown' and another first try at the only song to remain unpublished: 'Julius and Ethel'

Of all of them, 'I And I' seems to have been invested with a most personal story. One can picture the bed, the room, the sleeping figure, the road, the train tracks. The listener "seeing" the scene is enhanced in part because the music, not quite reggae, not quite rock ballad, pulls him or her in that direction.

The first recorded evidence began as instrumental warm-ups. Dylan sang the first verse and chorus, and directed how he wanted Knopfler to play. "That's the chord, sounds alright," he said. The bass and bass drum were heavy at this time, the piano was light.

The third verse was set in past tense—"didn't win the race, it went to the worthy." He reverted to an image from the notebook of "walking through the wilderness." After the last verse, Dylan stated that he could not sing the song by himself and needed some help.

It was a passing thought, since no one else sang during the following takes.

Each of the musicians spent the following nine minutes practicing their possible backings for this atmospheric song. Knopfler experimented with delay on his guitar, and commented, "Piano's great."[175] "Gonna be great," Knopfler enthused after a bit more warmup.

Dylan experimented with an extended harmonica intro. When he complained that his guitar sounded like a "rubber band," Knopfler told him not to worry about it. They worked on sections of the song, and Dylan sang the verses with little space in-between them. Knopfler noticed they needed to decide the space between verses and again said it was going to be great. Dylan said it as well.

Bob asked to take it from the top and polled the musicians about their satisfaction. He decided against a harmonica intro and laughed. They decided on the short percussion intro, and the master take was put down. The archives recording includes a Dylan synth overdub, some of his guitar overdubs and other elements from June 6 and 7. Somewhere on the multitrack are overdubs from Ron Wood, but they were not brought forward. Neither was a B-3 organ part. The "smoking' down the track" vocal insert was double tracked. An aborted additional chorus included "walking through the meadowland." The take is noted as the master.

Future engineers and mix specialists could play with a lot of music on the 32 tracks and they did on the version submitted for copyright and on the later Reggae version released on *Is It Rolling Bob?-A Reggae Tribute to Bob Dylan* from 2004, produced by Dr. Dredd.

Dylan starts riffing, "True something, a truism. (Sings) Tell me what is truer than true, oh tell me what is truer than true. Tell me, if it's you. I gave my love a cherry without a stone, I gave my love a rainbow without a home. (Sighs) Ah, yeah."

A final take on a new reel of tape had a beginning that is predictive of sound on 1989's 'Man in the Long Black Coat'. This take of 'I And I' was slightly faster and had church-like organ backing rather than piano. The words were changed to "I got nothing to say about what could and could not be." Dylan's harsher delivery for this version stripped the song of the questioning mystery of the previous takes. At the conclusion, Dylan said "I've had it with that I think. Maybe we can do it better and maybe we can't but that's always the story."

The song was performed a respectable 204 times between 1984 and 1999 and has been put away for the past 20 years.

175 / In the November 5, 2018 interview, Clark felt his contribution was a key element in the song

17:

Julius and Ethel

No Published Lyrics
Julius and Ethel

Writing

'Julius and Ethel' has apparently been assigned to Dylan-limbo. It's one of the rare songs that, while submitted for copyright and long-circulating on bootlegs, has not been officially published. Nor does it seem to have been recorded by any other artist, which allows it to remain unpublished.

Certainly the subject matter—two Americans born in Manhattan and living in Brooklyn who were convicted of espionage on behalf of the Soviet Union and subsequently executed—is controversial. Julius and Ethel Rosenberg remain the only Americans executed for espionage during the Cold War. Dylan's telling of the story is weak history, but Dylan has never claimed to be a historian. He built the stories he wished to tell on foundations that included some basic facts upon which he then constructed his own narrative. He told the story and supplied the moral consideration with which he wished to leave the listener. 'The Lonesome Death of Hattie Carroll' was not a verbatim transcript of events. Neither was 'Hurricane' or 'George Jackson' or 'Lenny Bruce' or 'Joey'. Most recently, the 2012 'Roll On John' was built on the outlines of John Lennon's story but was not a biography.

Details have emerged about the Rosenberg case from the 1995 declassification of broken Soviet codes gathered by the ultra-secret project codenamed Venona. Further information has come from access to Soviet archives opened since the fall of that regime in 1992. Copious evidence, which the US Government kept secret at the time of trial, demonstrates that Julius was engaged in efforts to supply Russia with secret information. He also recruited other people to spy for the Soviet cause.[176] Whether secrets about the atomic bomb were included—or useful—is not conclusive. The level of Ethel's involvement is not conclusive and remains debated. Did she know what Julius was doing? Did she type up notes to help? There is little argument that the prosecution capitally charged Ethel as a tool to break Julius and get him to confess and identify others. The game of chicken concluded with execution, with the couple silently willing to leave their two small children behind.

176 / Haynes, John Earl and Harvey Kiehr. Venona: *Decoding Soviet Espionage in America*. Yale University Press, 2000

The case against Ethel was tainted because a key witness for the government was the Rosenberg's brother-in-law, David Greenglass. He did make bomb drawings which he claimed he passed on to Julius. Today, evidence indicates he testified that Ethel committed actions actually attributable to his own wife Ruth, Ethel's sister.

With the Rosenberg case, which arose when Bob Zimmerman was nine and concluded when he was 12, there were Jewish-Americans who believed (and still believe) that the couple were subjected to the harshest of prosecutions and penalties because of their religion. Some, including the Rosenberg's two sons, perceive that as the case to this day.[177]

Whether Dylan carried an awareness of the case from boyhood or whether his time in Brooklyn with the Lubavitchers prodded his memory and thinking, we do not know. Certainly, in 1983, the information secret in Soviet archives and American classified documents was not available to provide a broader picture. In writing that was left out of the liner notes for *Planet Waves*, Dylan noted similar hysteria at different times of the nation's history: "Dirge for dying America – for the dream gone cold...Haymarket Square, Sacco & Vanzetti, Ethel and Julius...4 dead in Oh-High-oh."[178]

Along with 'Neighborhood Bully', 'Julius and Ethel' at least hints at being concerned with the perception and treatment of Jewish people in the world, the Middle East and America. 'Julius and Ethel' and 'Clean-Cut Kid' (Brooklyn Anthem) both aim at the facade constructed of American life in the Fifties. Perhaps the main point of the song was Dylan's saying that any romantic notion of the Fifties was "a lie," and "As long as you didn't say nothing, you could say anything." This subject was compatible with the context of *Infidels*. It was not by any means a new subject for Dylan. His most comprehensive treatment of Fifties hypocrisy can be read in 'It's Alright Ma, I'm Only Bleeding'.[179]

177 / Meeropol, Robert and Michael Meeropol *We Are Your Sons: The Legacy of Julius and Ethel Rosenberg*. University of Illinois Press, 1986

178. / BDA, 2016.01.B89 F04

179 / Around the time he created 'It's Alright, Ma,' Dylan wrote a prose poem 'Advice For Geraldine On Her Miscellaneous Birthday', published in the program for his 1964 Halloween night Philharmonic Hall concert. It began "Stay in line, stay in step," which anecdotally is how he felt growing up in Fifties Hibbing, Minnesota. In filing for copyright for the poem, the publication date was given as October 31, 1964. 'It's Alright Ma' saw its fourth performance that night

In 'Julius and Ethel', Dylan flat-out claims, "they were never proven guilty beyond a reasonable doubt." Actually, so much has come out since they "are gone" that such a claim cannot hold up. They were, however, the "sacrificial lambs" he described. Saying, "Now that it is over no one knows how it began" expressed his view of the near mindless Red-hysteria that arose and dominated American politics for the 10 years following World War II.

One small part of 'Julius and Ethel' was on page 10 of the tan notebook Dylan likely carried in the Caribbean in January 1983. The phrase "He might do, just as he want/but not for as long as he like" corresponds to what follows "Every kingdom got to fall, even the third Reich" in the recorded outtake. Interestingly, considering the above theorizing on thematic connections with "Neighborhood Bully," those two words, 'Neighborhood Bully', are found on the same notebook page.[180]

In the written lyric folders in the archives, a Ritz-Carlton Hotel note pad has 'Julius and Ethel' written at the top and nothing relating to the song on the front side. On the back side, there may be some very tenuous connections via a reference or two to Brooklyn. A second hotel sheet has 'Julius and Ethel' at the top of the reverse side, but again nothing relating to the song.[181]

A single type-written draft has 17 verses for what ended up an eight-verse song. Extra lyrics dealt with electricity (and what it does to a body); the execution in the electric chair at Sing Sing Prison; fear of Communism; military spending; scapegoating; public apathy and the treachery of the Rosenberg's relatives. All were jettisoned, and in Dylan's corrections prior to a submission to the Copyright Office, he crossed out the opening lines of the verse about not saying anything.[182] A 3 x 5 inch card contains five of the 17 verses and one additional verse where the narrator questioned if "the land of the free....is just a memory."

180 / BDA, 2016.01.B99.F01 p. 10
181 / BDA, 2016.01.B36.F02, 01-02
182 / The original submission to the Copyright Office was on May 5, 1983, on four cassette tapes titled *Album 83*. Such a filing could be done in lieu of written lead sheets and lyrics. This method may have been chosen for speed and cost. This proved a mistake as three of the tapes were copied by a member of the public, and one of them was lost or stolen. *Empire Burlesque* was submitted in similar fashion and suffered a similar fate in that it was copied. All subsequent Dylan submissions have been made in writing. Written submissions were made for *Infidels* on January 20, 1984

Each two-line verse was followed by the three-line chorus that consists of 'Julius and Ethel' repeated.

Recording

During the April 27 session, Dylan broke off one of the takes of 'I And I' to begin a solo strum of 'Julius and Ethel', to give himself or his band a very rough feel for the beat. The strum resembled the 1984 live treatment of 'Tombstone Blues'. Robbie Shakespeare started playing along, and Alan Clark came in at the very end of the two minutes.

When Dylan finished working on 'I And I' he said, "Let's try this one song here. It's really simple. Mick, you should play that Gibson I think. Yeah...ok. Make it fast." The archive tapes have one partial run-through of the up-tempo rocker, and one complete blazing track. Both have a Farfisa organ dubbed onto them, and the 5:54 final had some other strange Prophet synthesizer sounds added. Clydie King duetted on the choruses. The additions seem to have been done at the initial recording date of April 27. Harmonica tracks on the multitrack are not audible on the archive mix. An engineer noted, "the drier the better," on the track sheet, which could have been a direction from Dylan. A more stripped-down mix is on the "Compiled Master #2" that was the basis for the cassettes submitted for copyright.

Had it been included on *Infidels*, 'Julius and Ethel' would have been the most straight-forward rock and roll song on the album.

CHAPTER 17 / JULIUS AND ETHEL

18:

Lord Protect My Child

Published Lyrics
Lord Protect My Child[183]

1	For his age, he's wise
2	He's got his mother's eyes
3	There's gladness in his heart
4	He's young and he's wild
5	My only prayer is, if I can't be there
6	Lord, protect my child
7	As his youth now unfolds
8	He is centuries old
9	Just to see him at play makes me smile
10	No matter what happens to me
11	No matter what my destiny
12	Lord, protect my child
13	The whole world is asleep
14	You can look at it and weep
15	Few things you find are worthwhile
16	And though I don't ask for much
17	No material things to touch
18	Lord, protect my child
19	He's young and on fire
20	Full of hope and desire
21	In a world that's been raped and defiled
22	If I fall along the way
23	And can't see another day
24	Lord, protect my child

183 / Although the published lyrics have 'Lord, protect my child' at the end of each verse, the title does not have a comma. It may be a scrivener's error

25   There'll be a time I hear tell
26   When all will be well
27   When God and man will be reconciled
28   But until men lose their chains
29   And righteousness reigns
30   Lord, protect my child

Writing

During five weeks in the archives in Tulsa, I failed to uncover any draft lyrics for 'Lord Protect My Child'.

A written version Dylan corrected for copyright purposes had him remove a second "raped" in line 21. The uncorrected version was presumably transcribed from the selected recorded track of the song. This was released on *The Bootleg Series Vol. 1-3: Rare and Unreleased* as it was recorded: "In a world that's been raped, raped and defiled." The 2016 Lyric book has the line as Dylan directed. The large *2014 Lyrics* has it as recorded.

There is a very tenuous connection to the second line and a thought in the tan notebook: "He said, 'Hey baby you got nice eyes.' She said 'thank you—tell my mother.'" Not much, but the "mother's eyes" survived when Dylan wrote this song.

The song was sung as a prayer for a child. There is a draft, seemingly from this period, of another prayer/song for the writer himself."[184]

The world depicted in 'Lord Protect My Child' is the one overrun with the evil portrayed throughout *Infidels*. On the surface, 'Lord Protect My Child' appeared to be a plea for one of Dylan's own sons. The release of the album had been delayed, possibly in order to use a photograph on the back cover of Dylan on a Jerusalem hillside.

A lot of "he's" appear in the lyrics: "He's got his mother's eyes....He's young and he's wild...He is centuries old....he's young and on fire." Dylan used the words "he" or "he's" thirty- five times in '"Neighborhood Bully'. In 'License To Kill', the words are used six times. Of course, in 'Man of Peace', there are twelve uses, so pointing all this out really proves nothing.

184 / 2016.01.B81.F03.01

And, as always with a Dylan song, we should be cautious of what seems obviously direct and personal on the surface.

Although the album may have been recorded digitally, the production thinking was still geared toward the limitations of the vinyl format (CD's were essentially newborns), where the released 52 minutes pushed the technical envelope. Had the release come two years later, perhaps the extra 25 minutes afforded by the CD would have permitted this and other songs to present the complete vision of a raped world and men in chains.

Recording

The long, long May 2 session produced six complete takes of 'Lord Protect My Child'. It was the first song recorded that day and was done at three distinct times in between 'Angel Flying Too Close To The Ground', 'Union Sundown' and 'Green Green Grass of Home'."It was followed by 'Death Is Not The End'.

The lyrics and melody were set from the start, and Dylan did not tinker with anything other than the tempo and accompaniment.

The first attempts began with Dylan playing rudimentary guitar and singing off mic. A Leslie speaker was briefly on the organ and Dylan may have taken a short run on the bass. A full instrumental rehearsal was far more guitar dominated than the piano-drum-guitar combination that evolved. There was some wonderful slide-dobro. The next take was a run-through vocal taken in a bouncier fashion than the familiar released version. A church-like organ and picked guitar dominated the instruments. The next try was still a choppy treatment. Clark seems to be at the piano for this one. The harmonica and guitars and bass wove around each other in the break before the final verse. Choppy or not, it was a fine version. The melody, though, is so reminiscent of 'License To Kill' that it is hard to imagine both songs on the same album. Dylan noticed the similarity, "We already used that chord." The run tape shows continued rehearsal featuring dobro. Dylan sang as the song proceeded in a country-gospel style. Immediately after this rehearsal for 'Lord Protect My Child' was finished, Dylan began singing 'Angel Flying Too Close To The Ground'.

The group picked up again on 'Lord Protect' after preliminary takes of 'Angel'. Dylan tried a 3/4 time signature. Bob assured himself it was recorded as Mark said, "That isn't bad. That's good singing, right Neil?" Dylan then wanted to play cross-harp on the song and wanted to take it from the top. Clark moved to piano for the next take. A much-slowed down treatment is tried for a minute-and-a-half, but the beat was hard to maintain. "Let's not get carried away with this thing," Dylan said, "It's got to be held back. What happened to the dobro? It was a nice one." Knopfler said he had put it away. Another well-sung version was put down, but Dylan felt it was too fast. The next take started with a 'Tumblin' Dice' lead-in.

Dylan moved to a 2/4 beat, and slowed the song down. He then followed with a few verses sung in a very bluesy fashion, and gradually the piano part evolves into what will be released.

The (officially) fourth take started with Dylan saying, "Go ahead Alan," and was essentially—in combination with the sixth take—what wound up on the released recording. Dylan said, "I think it's got to be in there." It was rightfully marked, "very good," and, "Bob likes," on the sheet.

The group was on the third reel of the day and did two more takes, better, including Dylan doing a long harp intro almost identical to 'License to Kill'. Bob's singing on the take was probably he strongest vocal for the song. "We want to do that again," Dylan insisted, and he was looking for "something specific on guitar for the third line, Clark said. "Every time we do it, it sounds great, but we never get it right." Dylan felt an A minor "belongs in there somewhere." They did one more take and went on to, as Dylan called it, "That 'Union' thing."

They came back later for a final try. A soft harmonica led the final take. The sheet noted, "Bob loves w/4," and fortunately the rough mix in the archives allows both vocal tracks to be heard. There were still Dylan vocal overdubs, the Farfisa and bass redos in the song's future. However, the finished track seems to differ very little from the fourth take.

CHAPTER 18 / LORD PROTECT MY CHILD

179

19:

Death Is Not the End

Published Lyrics
Death Is Not the End

1   When you're sad and when you're lonely

2   And you haven't got a friend

3   Just remember that death is not the end

4   And all that you've held sacred

5   Falls down and does not mend

6   Just remember that death is not the end

7   Not the end, not the end

8   Just remember that death is not the end

9   When you're standing at the crossroads

10   That you cannot comprehend

11   Just remember that death is not the end

12   And all your dreams have vanished

13   And you don't know what's up the bend

14   Just remember that death is not the end

15   Not the end, not the end

16   Just remember that death is not the end

17   When the storm clouds gather 'round you

18   And heavy rains descend

19   Just remember that death is not the end

20   And there's no one there to comfort you

21   With a helpin' hand to lend

22   Just remember that death is not the end

23   Not the end, not the end

24   Just remember that death is not the end

25   Oh, the tree of life is growing

26   Where the spirit never dies

27   And the bright light of salvation shines

28 In dark and empty skies

29 When the cities are on fire
30 With the burning flesh of men
31 Just remember that death is not the end
32 And you search in vain to find
33 Just one law-abiding citizen
34 Just remember that death is not the end
35 Not the end, not the end
36 Just remember that death is not the end

Writing

Four draft versions of 'Death Is Not the End' exist, three of which are complete. It was an *Infidels* song from birth. Despite rumors of being an extra track for the cassette version of *Infidels*, the song did not gain release until 1988 when it appeared on the final mutation of *Down In The Groove*.[185]

It was the last original composition introduced in the recording sessions...and it's somber delivery and gloomy lyrics would have fit the mood, while not the commercial appeal, had it concluded the album. Dylan was presenting the belief in the lyrics that there is a world beyond this, so there is always something to look forward to. But maybe what's beyond death isn't necessarily good. Perhaps the "bright light of salvation" will shine only on the worthy. That is not stated, but perhaps is implied. But certainly no one would enjoy "cities... on fire with the burning flesh of men."

As he was writing what would evolve into 'Someone's Got A Hold Of My Heart', Dylan wrote the burning fire image, flesh of men and searching for a "law abiding citizen" thoughts off to the side of one page, along with "when the seas begin to boil and the stars above descend." He could have already been working on "'Death Is Not the End' on other pages and simply was capturing a thought.

Many religions have an end-of-days" component in their belief systems, not always in the mainstream of the faith. Dylan's expounding on the concept

185 / *Down in the Groove* was honored by *Rolling Stone* as Dylan's worst album. The track listing went through three different groups of songs before it was finally released, with an "incorrect" lineup released in Argentina

in a song may or may not have been tied to his previous explorations with Christianity. It could have been part of a completely personal belief system and more recent interviews indicate it could still be.

Two complete drafts are similar. One has some additional ideas for a verse between verses three and four: "When peace of mind you cannot buy back/no matter what you spend," also "when despondency takes root, it's awful arms extend" and "...appointment is set / and you know where or when."

The third draft revises line 10 to "where time & space extend." Lines 17 and 18 are "When voices sound like buzzsaws / & all backstabbers say 'Amen.'" The storm cloud lines appear at the bottom of the page.

Some of the thoughts and words are also found on a song that started out as 'Life's Too Short', and is placed by the archives with the other three drafts. The theme was basically that there was no time to waste: "ain't got time to shoot the breeze/ain't got time to tease." The would-be song quickly devolves into written thoughts, including an observation that it is good that McDonalds is doing well selling hamburgers because "no business on judgement day."

Elements of 'Death Is Not The End' are here and there on the page, including the future title itself. The sad/weary, bright light of salvation, and tree of life are among the writing.

Although placed fourth in the folder for the song's lyrics, it could be the first attempt.

Recording

It would have been an almost perfect conclusion to the recording sessions if this had been the final song. Alas, it was not "the end." May 2 concluded with more work on 'Angel Flying Too Close To The Ground'. And the basic sessions did conclude on May 5, for two go's at 'Blind Willie McTell'. Then came overdubs, more overdubs, mixing, mastering. So the end is rarely the end.

'Death Is Not the End' is, for all intents and purposes, a one-take song. "Three verses, a bridge and that's it, out," Dylan says in the middle of three 50 second recordings before the full take. The bass drum has a tympani-like lowering boom. Bob announces he has to play harmonica, does so and then realizes they are rolling. "That's good," he says, "this is the hundredth song." Mick Taylor does not play on this track, which is a Dylan/Clydie King duet on the chorus. Dylan played guitar and later overdubbed guitar. On May 18, the Full Force R&B – Hip Hop vocalists[186] were brought in to overdub "no, no" on the chorus. The first of their two efforts was retained for the master.

The repetition of the chorus at the end gives a clue that the song may have been considered to close the album. The recording is cut off at the 7:24 mark, and the 5:08 released track misses the increasingly passionate delivery of the closing lines.

Had the song been included, indeed had it closed *Infidels*, some critical labeling of the work as a return to the secular might not have occurred. But there are quite a few "if only it" (pick your song) had been included" to ponder.

---

186 / Lucien J. George, Curtis Bedeau, Gerard Charles, Brian George, and Paul George. The also added backing vocals to 'Tell Me'

CHAPTER 19 / DEATH IS NOT THE END

20:

Prison Guard

No published lyrics, no known recording
Prison Guard

There are lyrics titled 'Prison Guard' with the *Infidels* material in The Bob Dylan Archive®[187]

21:

The Major
Covers

The Major Covers

Recording

During recording sessions, musicians routinely jam or do a few verses or so of familiar songs. Some of them are other artists' hits; some are obscurities dating to the earliest recorded music. The purpose can be to warm up, relax in the midst of more serious work or simply have fun playing music with other great musicians.

Dylan did plenty of this during the four weeks of recording *Infidels* at The Power Station.

He also made serious attempts to record full versions of other artists' songs. One of them, Willie Nelson's 'Angel Flying Too Close To The Ground', was released as the "B" side of 'Union Sundown' in several international markets.

'This Was My Love' was the first cover given serious treatment, initially as a single try on April 14. It was written by James Herbert and recorded by Frank Sinatra in 1959 for the Capitol album *No One Cares*[188].

The April 14 recording was a one-off. The vocal is not a committed "for a take" effort. It's a soft song recorded in between the faster, harder 'Clean-Cut Kid' and 'Man of Peace'. On April 19, perhaps, an acoustic guitar plucks the melody, which is not even noted on the sheets the engineers filled out. I say perhaps April 19 because the preceding song was noted as "4/20. The top of the sheet has "4/19" noted in the slot for the date. So, either they started afresh on April 20 with the preceding day's reel, which seems unlikely; or the session went past midnight.

The next take, on April 20 and on a new reel and had a 12-string plucking the melody. In the middle, Dylan asks, "How do you feel? Tired?" He played on and the other musicians followed as he emphasized the bridge on the 12-string. Very little singing was done. At the end, he asked Mick if he wanted to play piano.

After a pair of Robbie and Sly rhythm pieces, they all returned to 'This Was My Love'. Organ and piano sound indicate that Taylor may well have given it a turn on the keyboards. The minute-and-a-half try had Dylan singing in falsetto and noting it was not the right key. Things got more serious on the following

188 / The 1959 album's songs would be mined beginning in 2014 for Dylan's so-called Sinatra albums. In 1967, Sinatra changed the words to 'This Is My Love' and recorded it for his Reprise label's *The World We Knew*

take. Whoever was playing the piano gave a Floyd Kramer treatment. Clark was possibly on the piano as whoever was at the organ produced rudimentary chords. Knopfler was Knopfler, and he dressed the song with lovely fills The take evolved into a focused rehearsal for a song considered for the album. The key on this take was still too high, and falsetto came in again to much laughter and the suggestion that it might take much overnight drinking to sing it that way.

Following a request for headphone sound levels to be lowered, rehearsal settled on a key Dylan was pleased with (although he still strained at the close of each verse), and Knopfler said. "sounds great." Dylan determinedly remained with the 12-string, plucking out parts during an instrumental section. Two more complete takes wrapped up the real work on 'This Was My Love', with the middle of the three marked "good." A reggae coda minute of the song put it to bed.

The song was not chosen for inclusion when the safety master was compiled. Two mixed versions of the last two complete takes appeared on bootleg albums, but whether the mixing was done in the studio is doubtful.

'Across The Borderline' was written in 1982 by Jim Dickinson, John Hiatt and Ry Cooder. It was used in the movie *The Border*, starring Jack Nicholson. Dylan wrote out the lyrics so he'd have the words correct when he sang the song during the April 20 session. This conveyed a greater level of importance than many of the other covers during the month of recording. Even so, after two rehearsals, Dylan did a full recording of the song, commented, "It's kind of tricky" and ended recording for the day. 'Across the Borderline' stayed alive for Dylan. He performed it in February 1986 early in his tour with Tom Petty and The Heartbreakers, on national television for *Farm Aid* 1986 and sporadically in his sets up to November 1998. He played it 57 times.

There is an interesting cross-fertilization with Dylan and Cooder and others involved in 'Across The Borderline's' history. Cooder included 'I Need A Woman', an outtake from *Shot of Love*, on his on 1982 album *The Slide Area* and played guitar on 'Clean Cut Kid' for Carla Olson and the Textones in 1984.[189] Dylan recorded John Hiatt's song 'The Usual' for the movie *Hearts of Fire* in 1986. Jim Keltner, Dylan's drummer from 1979-1981, recorded with Cooder and Hiatt. Dylan featured Ry Cooder at least three times on his *Theme Time Radio Hour* series, including

189 / Carla Olson played the part of Mick Taylor in the video for 'Sweetheart Like You'

'Across The Borderline' in the first season's 44th episode, *Texas*. Looking back with 2019 perspective, I find it interesting that Dylan commented on his radio show that in a seven-month period from October 2003, 660,000 people were detained at the Texas-Mexico border for crossing illegally.

'Choo Choo Boogie', recorded by Louis Jordan & His Tympani Five, had an 18-week run atop the R&B charts in 1946. It was written by Vaughn Horton, Denver Darling and Milton Gabler. Gabler was a Vice President of Decca Records and, besides managing Jordan, produced Bill Haley's 'Rock Around the Clock'. Haley subsequently recorded 'Choo Choo Ch-Boogie' in 1956, and there is a good likelihood that the record would have been heard by 15-year-old boys in Hibbing, Minnesota.

'Choo Choo Boogie' (or 'Ch-Boogie') is very similar to 'Boogie Woogie Bugle Boy' in structure. It was one of three songs Dylan selected for double vocal treatment on April 26. The other two were 'Cold, Cold Heart' and Clarence (Hank) Snow's 'I'm Moving' On'. Snow's version was released in May 1950 and spent a record 21 weeks at Number One on Billboard's Country Music charts.

The three songs were marked "double vocal" at the time they were recorded (although the other vocals were most likely added on May 17, when Clydie King (Claudia on one sheet) overdubbed. It is tempting to speculate that the three were not intended for *Infidels*, but rather for an ongoing Dylan-King project discussed by Bob around this time. Indicating a more serious effort than just session goofing around are sheets delineating the 24-tracks used. Such is not the case for many of the one-off numbers played during the weeks of sessions.

'Angel Flying Too Close To The Ground' was written by Willie Nelson. It appeared in the movie *Honeysuckle Rose* and was Nelson's seventh Number One Billboard Country hit. On May 2, Dylan devoted five complete takes, after considerable rehearsal, to get the song suitable for release, which it was as a 'B' side for a number of singles from *Infidels* in overseas markets.

Dylan records a number of takes of 'Angel', and says to Knopfler, "I think it's in there somewhere. What do you think, Mark?" Knopfler responds, "Kind of nice. I think Ronnie will like it." "Ronnie who," Bob asks. "Mark says, "Willie. Who wrote that?" Bob finishes with, "Merle Haggard, I don't know." He then turns his attention to completing 'Lord Protect My Child' and 'Union Sundown', as well as the essentially one-and-done 'Death Is Not The End'. He then wants to go back to try 'Angel Flying Too Close To The Ground' "as long as we're here." It sounds like Clydie King is in the studio at this point, as the interchanges seem of the moment as opposed to an overdub. Before they begin on the song again, Dylan says, "For all the girls at the Sarora tea house. Everybody from Austin, Texas, if they still live in Austin, Texas."

The final take is chosen for the single "B" side, following mixing and considerable overdubs for Dylan's harmonica, Farfisa and guitar parts. The speed is altered slightly on the single.

Between the start and finish of takes of 'Angel Flying Too Close To The Ground', one more duet with Clydie King is laid down, again a former Country Music hit, 'Green, Green Grass of Home'. The lyrics portray the happy homecoming dream of a prisoner as he wakes on the day of his execution. Yes, he would be returning home, but he realizes as he becomes fully alert that he is still in prison and the guards and the priest will soon be coming for him.

The song was written by Claude "Curley" Putnam Jr.[190] and covered by many. The first hit was courtesy of Porter Waggoner in 1965. Tom Jones heard Jerry Lee Lewis' version and recorded his own, which hit Number One in the UK in 1966.

The musicians rehearsed and completed two takes, and Knopfler observed "Not as good as Tom Jones." Dylan disagreed, "No, no, it's a hundred times better than Tom Jones." He dedicated the song, "For Barbados." The Dylan-King duet of this song has long been yearned for in its absence by fans, and it is a good and heartfelt rendition.

---

190 / Putnam also wrote 'He Stopped Loving Her Today', 'D-I-V-O-R-C-E' and is in the Nashville Songwriters Hall of Fame

CHAPTER 21 / THE MAJOR COVERS

22:

Covers, Jams, Noodles, Etc.

Covers, Jams, Noodles, etc

In the month of sessions for *Infidels,* quite a bit of playing captured on tape was not intended for the serious work of recording songs for the album. It was work, nonetheless, as whether it was for fun, relaxation, trying a lick or just goofing around, it helped prepare Dylan and the musicians for actual takes.

This chapter will present each day's lighter work. This will be reconciled in Appendix 4, which will outline each day's session from start to finish. The engineers' sheets, Michael Krogsgaard's session history and the archive tapes do not match. Therefore, for purposes of this book, I have relied on what is actually on the tapes (times are track duration).

April 11

Rundown 4:21 Dylan pounded the piano, others joined in; sounds like 'Six Days on the Road'.

Rundown 5:36 just playing

Rundown 6 :33 bluesy

Rundown 7:01 organ added to the instruments, Dylan faintly singing a bit of 'Jokerman' off- mic

Rundown Piano 7:45 Dylan repetitive piano riff with Taylor now noticeable

Rundown 8 vocal tryout 4:28 vocal in question was 'Jokerman', very highly pitched and taken at a tempo reminiscent of 'Take It Easy'.

Rundown piano 9:57 Dylan playing chords for 'Blind Willie McTell', harmonica off mic at the three-minute mark. After four minutes, a tempo shift to what would become the familiar beat of the song. A vocal began almost seven minutes in. This "rundown" evolved into a rehearsal for the session's first formal take, which began on the next reel. Nearly ten minutes fit the description of Dylan sessions where songs and arrangements come about organically.

'Oh Babe' 7:40 This was a minor key, march-like piece populated with dummy lyrics throughout, each "verse" ending in "oh, babe, yeah babe." A breather for the group between work on takes of 'Blind Willie McTell' and a chance for Dylan to do some rock vocals.[191]

Instrumental Jam - 3:10 Very close to jazz, with Knopfler, Clark and Dunbar leading the way.

April 13

Slow 'Try Baby' 6:02 It sounds like a song, it wants to be a song, but it's not a finished work. 'Try Baby' has a Fats Domino-style piano by Dylan but dummy lyrics: "You got fools, fools on the right; you got fools on the left, you got lost. Try baby, try baby, try love."

Blues 2:06 Just that, a blues with improvised lyrics in places.

'Columbus Stockade Blues' 2:15 A Jimmy Davis song, most famously sung by Doc Watson.

'A Couple More Years' 1:37 Written by Dennis Locorriere of Dr. Hook and Shel Silverstein. It served as a go-to song for Dylan for a few years. He performed it in his December 1980 shows and also recorded it during the sessions for *Hearts of Fire*. At the end of this brief recording Dylan said, "You didn't take that, I hope."

'Do-Re-Mi' 3:28 Dylan revisited Woody Guthrie on this piano-backed run through.

---

191 / The work on 'Blind Willie McTell' on this first day of recording finishes the second reel of tape with what is known as the full-band version of the song

Blues 7:43 This is a blues recording begun with Dylan asking to hear Mick and the two duetted on guitar and harmonica. At five minutes in, Dylan began to play some piano and sing a couple of words.

April 14

The engineer's sheet (and thus Krogsgaard) shows "Rainbow/This Was My Love." However, there is nothing on the tape here but "This Was My Love."

April 15

'He'll Have To Go' 1:16 The engineers had this as the first of two 'Don't Fly Unless It's Safe' takes. "He'll Have To Go" was written by Joe and Audrey Allison and was a hit in the fall of 1959 for Jim Reeves. It crossed over from country to the pop charts as Dylan was beginning his freshman, and only, year at the University of Minnesota. The 1983 recording is a sweet, albeit brief, instrumental.

'Don't Fly Unless It's Safe' 5:58 Dylan had a definite melody for this instrumental song that he was playing on the piano as the others filled in. No words have ever been associated with it.

'Jesus Met The Woman At The Well' 4:12 Dylan gave the traditional gospel song a stop/start vocal and piano treatment.

'Half-Finished Song' 0:55 Dylan played about a minute then asked if the others could do it.

'Half-Finished Song' 3:20 The answer must have been "yes," and Dylan called it "Half-Finished Song" and wanted it saved for his future consideration. He was playing (probably without realizing it) what is basically 'When I Paint My Masterpiece'.

'16 Tons' 6:50 This is a downward chord progression, bluesy treatment of an essential mining song, attributed to Merle Travis (with some dispute). Many, many have covered the song including Tom Jones on his *Green, Green Grass of Home* album (See previous chapter), which also had "He'll Have To Go." Dylan

had a good time playing the piano on the song, which moved into jazz. Dylan even called out "Brubeck" as he jammed.[192] At the conclusion, Dylan said "16 Tons...you guys ever heard that." He was enthusiastic about it.

'It's Too Late (She's Gone)' 4:02 A 1956 hit for Chuck Willis, the recording cut in during discussion among Dylan and the musicians about how it went. No connection to Dylan's 'Too Late' from these sessions.

'The Circle Game' 0:37 Yes, it's the Joni Mitchell song. It was not on the track sheet.

'Sitting In Limbo' 1:50 Also not written down on the track sheet, this is the Jimmy Cliff song.

All the songs from April 15 have Dylan on piano.

April 16

'People Get Ready' 4:27 Noted on the sheet as "Bluesy Jam: Slow."

'Bluesy Jam: Bluesier' 18:17 Dylan and the crew used two reels of $90 digital tape while warming up for the one new Dylan song they would work on that day, 'Someone's Got A Hold Of My Heart'. 'Bluesy Jam' is a repetitive chug-a-lug riff that would be meandering if it ventured anywhere beyond its limited boundaries dominated by bass.

'Pickup Again' 9:13 Not exactly a continuation of the previous track, the piano and guitar strived to create a melodic framework. Dylan was probably playing rhythm guitar. Taylor was credited on piano.

'Da Da Da Grateful Dead' 5:22 Without any vocalized instructions, there is no

---

192 / Dave Brubeck was a major figure in late-Fifties early Sixties jazz. A label-mate of Dylan's on Columbia Records, he had pioneering works in unconventional time signatures. HIs quartet's influential 1959 *Time Out* was the rare jazz recording that reached Number 2 on Billboard and was a platinum-seller

way of knowing what the Dead might have to do with the track. The beat was in fact da da da, da da da, da da da. The engineers noted "Keep this Bob."

'Reggae Toms Toms Jam' 8:20 More repetitive rhythmic jamming, not definitively reggae.

"Bob said tape this" 7:08 Dylan might have had some idea for what this might be someday, but what it might be is difficult at best for the mortal mind to grasp. Again, an unvarying "jam."

"Mark Soop Pick Up" 4:32 Seemed to be a test of sounds for Knopfler's guitar. It is a prototype for 'Dark Groove', which would be its own track a little later.

'Oh Sussanah' 2:13 Not the Stephen Foster minstrel song 'Oh Susana'. More 'Dark Groove'.

This was followed by six minutes of jamming at the end of one reel and the beginning of the next, which are not noted on the engineer sheets. One guitar, probably Dylan's, had a clanging tone.

'Dark Groove New Toon' 9:19 Dylan was a bit more inventive in what he was playing, and there was some very interesting drumming on the track.

'Dark Groove' (with organ) 0:58 Actually morphed into 'Someone's Got A Hold Of My Heart', of which a half-minute rehearsal ensued.

'Norwegian Wood' 0:38 This is not as exciting as it seems, merely guitar picking out melody line.

Six takes of 'Someone's Got A Hold Of My Heart' of varying lengths followed, interrupted by – *'Bob Picking' 0:37* This is self-explanatory.

'Boogie' 0:36

'Boogie' 3:16 A bluesy boogie, with all three guitarists evident.

'Mark Plucks Tasty' 5:04 They had to call it something.
Some unidentifiable playing goes on for about two minutes.

'Dark Groove' 5:27 This was the take that was on one of the copyright tapes bootlegged in the mid-Eighties. It had more development and chord changes than the earlier versions from the same day
.

Two minutes and forty-eight seconds of instrumental work completes the recordings for April 16. Four reels of tape were used and nary a vocal was heard.

April 19
'Just Run The Tape For a Minute On This Thing' 0:26 Bob instructed, engineer taped.

'Green Onions' 5:49 This take shared the bass and drum underpinnings with the Booker T & The MGs 1962 instrumental hit. But on this version, the guitars and organs deviated from the scale of the original.

'(Love You, Too)Jam' 8:16 A pleasant instrumental, but it is not clear if Dylan was playing on it or if the tune was his. There was some dissonant organ at the end that one suspects was Dylan.

'Trees Hannibal Alps' 15:41 A guitar picked out a repetitive riff, and it was echoed on a 12- string and mirrored by the piano. Not much can be said with authority for this nearly 16-minute jam, other that marveling, on this and all the others, how Dunbar and Shakespeare flawlessly maintained the beat. Of historical note, when Hannibal did cross the Alps in 218 B.C., there were probably some trees

The tape reel, and the day's recording, ended with some vague picking on a lone guitar.

April 20

'Robbie Sly Aquarium' 17:15 A workout for the two rhythm players. Robbie made some sliding sounds on his strings. An organ entered about five minutes in, guitar at six minutes, which sounds like Knopfler. At 10 minutes, keys on the piano were pounded, then tinkled. Effects on the guitar were experimented with, chunking sounds, waaaas and bubbling noises added to the extended jam. Despite the assigned title, this music would not be found on any actual aquarium sounds record.

'3G Boogie' 4:41 It is either '3G' or 'BG', the writing on both the tape box and sheet are unclear. The tune was not in G, and no one (except for Bill Graham) had the initials "BG." If 3G, perhaps three guitar.

April 22

Un-noted warmup 4:19 loosening up for work on 'Too Late'. Some limbering up of the fingers on piano.

'If I Give My Heart To You' 5:03 Dylan seemed to have a tune, possibly a cover, in mind, as he played piano. At the end it is revealed as the 1954 song by Milt Gabler, Jimmie Crane and Al Jacobs.[193]

Noodling with Tex-Mex feel 0:35

'Twelve Days of Christmas' 2:13 This began what some have concluded was Dylan's first attempt at a Christmas album. While he jokingly referred to such a thing and there were four holiday songs partially performed once at this point in the recording, it was studio goofing around. One of the musicians intrigued Dylan with a synthesizer effect Dylan asked about.

'Choo Choo Boogie' 5:00 A Milt Gabler composition (along with Vaughn Horton and Denver Darling) again appeared in the day's activities. The 1946 song

193 / See footnote 161 on page 144

reached number seven on national charts for Louis Jordan. Dylan seemed excited by the beat and the sound of the words and would revisit the song on April 26.

Jam with synthesizer and harp 0:39 Dylan asked "What Was That?" Exactly.

'Silent Night' 3:55 The classic song began with an indescribable synth sound, continued with harmonica soloing the first two verses as Knopfler followed the melody lines. Dylan provided a semi-falsetto vocal. "Alright," Bob said, "Got two songs for a Christmas album." He was JOKING!

'Glory To The King (Adestes Fidelis)' 0:35 The recording picked up only the last part of what seems to have been a longer version. Dylan asked for "lots of overdub on that, too."

'Lovers Concerto' 2:03 Sandy Linzer and Denny Randell wrote this song, a record for The Toys that sold two million copies, reached number 2, and was topped only by the Beatle's 'Yesterday' for the top spot. It is based on Bach's 'Minuet in G Minor'. (Top Ten love and theft?) Dylan cut off Knopfler's beginning 'Good King Wenceslas' to recall the Concerto. He admitted he'd have to get the record to learn the words.

'Dark As A Dungeon' 2:53 "Merle Travis'...you'll like it," as Bob continued to call out songs.

This is the last for April 22. Perhaps the final reels reflected time taken for needed relaxation or putting off work to get 'Too Late' the way he thought it should be.

April 23

Jam with Piano 3:25 A breather between work on 'Too Late;, not notated on sheets.

April 26

Vocal Overdubs(Run-in') 3:15 Dylan seemed to be putting something down for future use as he asked Josh Abbey to make a note of it. The drum part is similar to 'Man of Peace'.

'Wildwood Flower' 0:47 The recording sheet says 'Prison Station Blues', but there is no mistaking the song.

Mark picking 0:17 And delighting a laughing Dylan.

'Wildwood Flower' 0:58 Same song, different try.

'Forever My Darling (Pledging My Love)' 1:30 Dylan was very familiar with the words for this song, possibly from Johnny Ace's 1954 hit. One might picture 13-year-old Bobby Zimmerman under his covers, keeping the late-night sounds from Shreveport low so his parents could not hear. Whether the imagined scene was real or not, he certainly knew the song. The nice moment was cut short when someone in the studio interrupted.

Following some work on 'Someone's Got A Hold Of My Heart', more non-Dylan was played.

'Choo Choo Boogie' (Part II) 2:32 The sound of the clickity clack once more, double vocals, with perhaps an overdubbed Clydie King.

'Cold, Cold Heart' 2:32 Somewhat properly associated with Hank Williams,[194] one of Dylan's "first idols."

'Cold, Cold Heart' 4:30 This song also had Dylan noting double vocal, but none can be heard on the Archive recording. The song was done at close to a bossa nova beat. Unfortunately, Dylan did not remember any more than a snippet of the lyrics.

---

194 / Somewhat properly, because Williams had the hit record and took credit for the writing. However, it is considered by some to have been purchased by Williams from Paul Gilley. Gilley also wrote 'I'm So Lonesome I Could Cry' and 'Crazy Arms'. He was 27 when he drowned in a swimming pool. Eerily, this fate fulfilled the final verse of Williams' 'Long Gone Lonesome Blues'

'I'm Moving On' 1:06 Rough practice on the Hank Snow classic. This song is an example of why artists snicker at record company executives. Snow, at his first recording session, proposed doing the song, but the supervisor turned it down. A year later, the same executive, possibly forgetting his earlier rejection, let it be recorded and released. It spent 21 weeks at #1 on the Billboard Country charts.

'I'm Moving On' 3:30 Multiple vocals, at least two of which are Dylan's, along with Clydie King. The Farfisa was on one of the 32 tracks, as well as an overdubbed harmonica. A lot of extra work on what ultimately got left behind.

'KIM' 3:43 Novak, Bassinger, North Korean dictator? No clue provided in the session information for this instrumental. It is by itself on a reel.

April 27
April 27 was the day 'Too Late' became 'Foot of Pride'.

'From Paul' 3:15 Around 2012, efforts were made to organize all Dylan session recordings. At that time, a researcher wrote "From Paul at Green." On the tape box and recording sheet and Dylan's spoken intro, it's only "From Paul." It is a pleasant enough instrumental.

April 29
After a rare Thursday off-day, work picked back up, work that would lock down 'Foot of Pride' once and for all. But there was time for three reels of warming-up, developing new prototypes for songs and having fun.

'Harmonica Jam' 4:20 This minor key number sounds vaguely familiar, almost like an Israeli folk song.[195]

'Harmonica Jam' 8:22 Another minor key, eastern European sounding melody. Dylan was trying to find a tune on piano and harp. Robbie Shakespeare and

---

195 / When played for an actual Israeli he did not recognize it

Sly Dunbar gamely tried to assist as the beat shifted. This and the two other 'Harmonica Jam' recordings were purely attempts at creation.

'Harmonica Jam' 10:01 Heavy tom-tom drum accompaniment. Dylan faintly sang a word or two. There were numerous tempo and key changes throughout the 10 minutes.

Deliberately or unknowingly, Dylan's harmonica traced the melody of 'My World Is Empty Without You Babe'. For aficionados of Dylan's harmonica work, these 22 minutes are a must

.

'Don't Drink No Chevy' 3:16 "I don't drink no Cadillac/I don't drink no Chevrolet/ Never liked the taste of the driver's seat/It just got in the way." Buick gets named in the next verse, but Dylan was simply riffing.

'Don't Drink No Chevy' 0:47 Work on the turnaround.

'Don't Drive No Chevy' 2:51 A marriage of the 'Harmonica Jams' and the melody of 'Don't Drink No Chevy'. Whatever Dylan had in mind, it is not realized in these sessions.

'How Many Days' 1:59 This sounds like the kind of Dylan minor-key song that might have been a classic if Dylan would have found lyrics to follow the repeatedly sung title.

'How Many Days' 6:32 Dylan also explored working with 'How many dreams' to begin verses. Dylan wanted this marked for reference. This was no goofing around, or killing time. It's a peek at embryonic song development. To echo the title, how many of these must there be over a nearly 60-year career? This one just happened to have been captured in a studio.

'Bluesy Riff' This was what was noted on the session sheets and in Krogsgaard, but there are really five separate groups of guitar riffs covering the final 15 minutes of one reel. On the fourth, Dylan contributed some harmonica. There are three

guitars audible, so Dylan is one of them. The final riff had a hip-hop beat.

'Mark Pickin'' *12:59* As Krogsgaard indicates, there is a word beginning with "gr" following "pickin'"on one sheet, although not on the tape box. Dylan was picking as well, back to the 'My World Is Empty Without You Babe' melody, which Knopfler began playing. Whatever the song was trying to become, Dylan and crew came back to it a number of times on April 29.

'Bob Lead Jazz' *1:20* Actually, a Knopfler/Dylan duet which turned into..... 'Home on the Range' 2:25 ....at least on Knopfler's part.

'Buttons and Bows' 2:05 This was written in 1947 by Jay Livingston and Ray Evans for a Bob Hope movie, *The Paleface*. Dinah Shore recorded the most popular version. Shore did at least drive (if not drink) a Chevy. When Dylan was inducted into the Songwriters Hall of Fame on January 24, 1982, photographer Lynn Goldsmith captured some charming shots of Dylan and Shore. Who can say whether this triggered the song popping up in this session? To be fair, it is Knopfler who began playing it.

'Gonna Wash That Man Right Outa My Hair' *0:35* Knopfler played Rodgers and Hammerstein (from *South Pacific*) while Dylan continued with 'Buttons and Bows'. The songs sounded good together.

'Great Buttons and Bows Again' *4:50* Dylan successfully picked out the melody line as Knopfler played jazz runs underneath, concluding with a few notes of 'There's Nothing Like A Dame', also from *South Pacific*.

The lengthy cover/instrumental work ended up with an instrumental portion of 'Foot of Pride', where Clark seems in evidence. If fact, neither Clark nor Taylor seem to have been in the studio until this point, and the rest of the day was devoted to finishing 'Foot of Pride'.

May 2

'Green Green Grass of Home' is mentioned in Chapter 21, but there are two minor recordings of it from May 2.

'Jam Groove' 1:18 Tried to break out in a Bo Diddley beat, but never quite did.

'Baby, What You Want Me To Do' 8:14 Despite Dylan having suggested 'Union Sundown', after some bars of that song, Dylan led them into the Jimmy Reed song, which the engineers write up as 'Goin' Up Let It Roll'. Taylor still tried some 'Sundown' licks, but Dylan prevailed with the Reed song. The vocal style harkens back to *New Morning*.

After this take, the rest of May 2 and May 5 are solely *Infidels*.

23:

Maybe,
Maybe Not

In The Bob Dylan Archive®, material is stored in file boxes. Boxes of lyrics are organized by years, with folders for lyrics of individual songs. This generally has served researchers well, as material for a given album, say *Infidels*, is relatively easy to locate in most cases. The archive is, at the time of this writing, being reorganized. As a result, items that had previously been grouped together may not be grouped the same way in the future.

As previously stated, Dylan did not date his writings. As a result, file boxes for *Infidels* lyrics also contain draft lyrics for songs that may or may not be from the *Infidels* period of composition and were not previously connected with *Infidels* – or for anything else for that matter.

Because of this uncertainty as to provenance of these writings and the ongoing reorganization of materials, this chapter will touch on lyrics and other writings contained in Boxes 35, 36, and 81, which otherwise definitely do contain lyrics from *Infidels*. No claim is made to definitively date when these were written, but they should be mentioned even if the possibility of the *Infidels* period may be remote. The future should provide greater clarity to what is now a mystery.

1. A 23-line amalgam of lyrics eventually appear in 'Death Is Not The End'. The words also reflect on the shortness of life and how the use of emotional responses must be measured with numbered days in mind. There is also a reflection on the success of McDonald's but notes "no business on judgement day." Finally, there are four unconnected lines about the necessity of faith "in the father of lights," without which no good can come. The writer notes an incident when the person being addressed "looked dracula straight in the eye."[196]

On a different sheet, the same thoughts are titled 'Ain't Got Time/Life's Too Short'. There is more structure to the rhythm and the verses are tighter: "Ain't got time to sweep you off your feet/or whip you when you wanna get beat/ain't got time to chase you up the street."[197]

2. While there are elements of 'Someone's Got a Hold of My Heart' on this sheet of writing – including the title – half of this page deals with a new awareness

196 / BDA,.2016.01 B35. F08 04
197 / BDA, 2016.01 B36 F09 01

of surroundings: birds singing "like never before;" a brighter sun; once straight things that are now crooked; an inability to see or hear what once was recognizable. This is summed up as "walking in a world of a living hell." This is preceded by an admonition (either to himself or others) not to believe all that's reported.[198]

3. On the reverse of lyrics for 'Julius and Ethel', a Ritz Carlton notepad has statements about the discomfort of being stared at; it was not how the writer was raised. In fact, when he "ran into Liz Taylor in an elevator and (he) wouldn't look at her." He rejects "all that John Wayne stuff— 'look 'em in the eye".[199]

4. This appears to be a song, and with a title at that 'I Can't'. Not surprisingly, it is a listing of things the writer cannot do for the person to whom it is addressed: touch the clouds or reach the sun; turn back time or turn barren fields to green; see the things she (presumably) hopes for. He knows perhaps someone else can meet her needs saying ,"I know your arms are open wide but Lord, wonder who they're open for."[200]

5. A song or poem that begins 'Look At Your Baby' points out the ways a person can be misled.[201] The words appear as a potential precursor to the thoughts that came on *Slow Train Coming*.

6. A song that begins 'Trouble in Twistedville', references James Joyce and Bloom and despairs of the doom that has been going on for a thousand years. "One of these days, man's gonna get it right and blow this world to tears."[202]

7. 'While Men Die of Hunger'. This is a three-and-a-half verse composition in the first of the *Water Pearl* notebooks. It immediately precedes a draft of 'I And I' and

198 / BDA,2016.01 B35 F07 07
199 / BDA, 2016.01 B36 F02 02
200 / BDA, 2016.01 B36 F06 02
201 / BDA, 2016.01 B36 F06 09
202 / 2BDA,016. 01 B81 F03

speaks of those who live a privileged life of riches while others are in need.[203]

These seven examples are the most developed of the many lines and couplets found within the archived material. To reiterate, there is no certainty that all are from the *Infidels* period.

24:

The Videos

During the month of sessions for *Infidels*, planning for some kind of video promotion for the project was set in motion. Albert and David Maysles[204] were hired to document the recordings on film, the results of which are in the archives as 90 minutes of silent black and white footage. Dylan and the musicians mime, mug and play unplugged instruments in varying combinations and go through at least one change of clothing. Although the participants appear to be enjoying themselves, viewing the footage is unrewarding. These are truly moving pictures.

Two prototype full-color videos from the studio sessions, possibly also filmed by the Maysles, were produced but not released. Lip-synched versions of 'Don't Fall Apart On Me Tonight' and 'License to Kill' were filmed at the Power Station. A Mick Taylor online database lists the films, with an unknown director, as being done in May.

For 'Don't Fall Apart on Me Tonight', the musicians seem to play the parts they have already recorded, with Robbie Shakespeare being particularly enthusiastic about the exercise. Mick Taylor is the most subdued of the group and is not in the foreground of the film. Dylan lip-synchs and pretend plays an electric guitar and harmonica. He also "sings" with his eyes open about 15 percent of the time, unlike in the 'Jokerman' video which will be filmed nearly a year later. That song was the take initially slated for the initial album release – until Dylan redid the vocal and some of the lyrics in June or July 1983.

'License To Kill' focuses more on Dylan, who has made a wardrobe change and sports a fashionable pre-Kangol-type cap. Dylan again lip-synchs to the recorded take.

A common story from the post-studio days is that Dylan had a concept for a video of 'Neighborhood Bully'. His idea was that a Sumo wrestler would basically wreak havoc in a locality. In July 1984, he told MTV's Martha Quinn that he envisioned American Wrestling Association's "Crusher" Jerry Blackwell in the role of the bully[205]: "I visualized 'Neighborhood Bully'... there were certain segments which I just wrote down one night which I thought would look great

---

204 / The Maysles Brothers were active as a partnership for more than 30 years until David's death in 1987. Their subject matter was broad and often reflected their training as psychologists. In the rock music area, they are known for *Gimme Shelter*, a film about the Rolling Stones 1969 tour of the United States. The tour culminated with a chaotically-executed free concert at Altamont Motor Speedway, during which one audience member was killed on camera
205 / Farinaccio, Vince Nothing To Turn Off 2007 p.158

on film and it would be like a Fassbinder movie."

If such a notion was actually considered, and not merely Dylan game playing with Quinn, such a concept could have served to confuse and deflect criticism that the song was overtly supportive of Israel.

Sweetheart Like You

The video promoting 'Sweetheart Like You' is noted on Internet Movie Database as being Dylan's "first official video of the MTV age." It was filmed at Culver City in Los Angeles in October 1983 and had its premiere on October 27. It was directed by Mark Robinson, who had previously worked on videos for Bob Marley, Tina Turner, Santana, The Ramones, The Pretenders and Pat Benatar.[206] Robinson states that he had a "good reputation" with CBS, parent of Columbia records. The record company had selected 'Sweetheart Like You' to be the first single from *Infidels* and wanted a video to promote the release. Debbie Newman was CBS' liaison for video.

"I had worked with Paul Cheslaw, who managed Tommy Tutone," Robinson remembered. "I had directed a video in 1981 for Tommy's song '867-5301/Jenny'." Paul had a friend, Gary Shafner, who worked with Bob Dylan and set up a meeting for me, Gary and Bob. Clydie King was there and Bob relied on her advice." (Note: This meeting was probably late July-early August.) " I was thrilled, we hit it off and agreed to do something," said Robinson. "CBS had selected the song that was going to become the video, and as we were establishing a budget, their concern was that Dylan was likely to abandon the effort once filming began. They wanted to know, 'How much was it going to cost if he quit in the first week, how much in the second week?'"

Dylan was involved in the creative decisions, production decisions and editing. However, trying to get to decisions "was like nailing Jello to the wall," according to the director. "The way I approached it was to give three options each for concept, wardrobe, staging, etc. This allowed for Dylan's unique creativity and also gave some structure to the process. When we actually shot, Dylan said, 'I want to wear what you're wearing', so that is my jacket in the video."

The original concept, as rumored in 1983, was for a number of women to

206 / Mark Robinson, FaceTime interview with author, May 23, 2019

214

portray the "Sweethearts." All would have on the same outfit but be different women. One idea was that each would morph into having the same face. "It was to be a performance piece," said Robinson, "with secondary interaction (with the women). But it just wasn't working." The decision was to have Dylan and the musicians perform the song to a single woman who would be cleaning up in a closed club.

There has been a lot of speculation over the years about the identity of the woman. One school of thought is that it was Dylan's mother, Beattie. Some think it's Dylan. "The casting was...she was just an actress with an interesting face," according to Robinson with no doubt or equivocation.

Dylan was there for almost all the filming, which was done by cinematographer Tom Ackerman (*Beetlejuice*). For a studio, Robinson used a space in a Culver City, California, industrial strip center. Shooting took a day, and filming was done on 35mm.

For the performance, Dylan is joined by Robbie Shakespeare on bass, Charlie Quintana[207] on drums, Steve Ripley on one guitar, with Carla Olson channeling Mick Taylor. Clyde King pretends to be on organ, and Greg Kuehn[208] is on piano. Dylan was in total control of how he looked, and, according to Robinson, was specific about his hair and makeup. The look itself is unlike any Dylan seen before or since. His hair is both poofed and down low on his forehead. And most odd, his eyebrows have been enhanced to the degree that the appearance is that of a werewolf the evening of a full moon. This significantly detracts and distracts from the story being presented (author's opinion).

Dylan remained involved in the cutting and the editing, even regularly calling Robinson at home. One specific cut at the end of the second bridge going into the verse about patriotism has a sudden jump to a more close-in shot. "That

207 / Charley Quintana was a member of The Plugz, a punk band that backed Dylan on his March 22, 1984, David Letterman appearance. Dylan was reported to have jammed with The Plugz at his Malibu home in late 1983 and into 1984. The archival *Infidels* run tapes include four reels dated October 20, 21 and 28, 1983. There are no vocals on the four hours of nearly formless playing and it sounds like Quintana on drums. These dates coincide with the time when the 'Sweetheart' video was filmed

208 / Kuehn was with a Los Angeles band T.S.O.L. Olson and Quintana were affiliated with Bill Graham's management company. Carlos Santana, a Graham artist, had worked with Mark Robinson on a video. Graham in fact was present at the production, remembered as holding court in a side room regaling listeners with biographical stories

was Bob's choice," said Robinson, who enjoyed working with Dylan despite the difficulty of aligning differing artistic visions. They did, however, discuss and agree on how to proceed.

Thirty-Five mm prints of the video were supplied to a number of movie theaters for promotional use, and there were reports from 1983-84 from those who were surprised to see it come on the screen.

As noted previously, Dylan has never performed the song in concert.

Jokerman

Dylan's second video from *Infidels* was released on March 27, 1984, five days after an energized appearance on *Late Night With David Letterman*, on which 'Jokerman' was performed in a shortened and newly arranged manner. Oddly, the song was not released as a single until June 1, more than two months later, possibly to tie in with the newly launched European tour. At any rate, it seems a strangely non-coordinated way to promote a song or album. Furthering the questionable promotion tactics, the flip side of 'Jokerman' was a live recording of 'Isis' from nine years earlier.

The co-producers of the video were Larry (Ratso) Sloman and George Lois. Sloman, met Dylan when he was a writer for *Rolling Stone* magazine and was invited to come on the Rolling Thunder Revue Tour. George Lois was a renowned advertising executive and had been the head of a committee to seek justice for imprisoned boxer Rubin "Hurricane" Carter and had interacted with Dylan to that end in 1975.

Both Sloman and Lois relate that the starting point was a call from promoter Bill Graham, who as noted previously, was presenting himself as Dylan's manager and in some areas acting "as if" while not formally holding such a post.[209] Both recall the opening as "I/we want Bobby to have a music video." Ratso maintains that Graham knew of Sloman's friendship with Lois and had him call up adman Lois to see if "you guys can come up with an idea." Lois remembers that call coming from Graham, not Sloman, and being told, "he(Dylan) hates videos, but if I told him you were doing it he would go along."

According to Sloman, the duo "took it like a homework assignment," listening

209 / Larry (Ratso) Sloman, FaceTime Interview with author, June 6, 2019; George Lois, phone interview with author, June 11, 2019

to the album together (Lois says independently), both agreeing immediately that 'Jokerman' was it. The idea was to "blow up Bob's lyrics in your face" and "intercut footage of Dylan with 5,000 years of art. "A poet should be read," according to Lois. So, "George storyboarded it," Ratso said, "and Dylan and Graham came up and were impressed." Lois quotes Dylan saying, "You know, George, I had a lot of these things (in mind) visually when I wrote it."

Lois worked on arranging the works of art to provide one illustration for the lyrics and coordinated with Dylan to assure his satisfaction.[210] (See Appendix 2 for list of art works.) One of the illustrated sequences for the line "shedding off one more layer of skin" showed photographs of Dylan from different time periods. When questioned, both Lois and Sloman said that the singer had no problem with such an unusually biographical depiction. "Never a peep," says Ratso.

Once the artwork was in place, with superimposed typography of the lyrics, a day was spent filming Dylan who was to lip-synch the chorus each time. Lois remembers, "Bob didn't understand why it had to be synched and refused to concentrate to match the recording properly. Sloman says that Dylan was nervous about the close-up and the synching, and Lois says that Dylan asked why the camera was so far away. Lois became exasperated and claims he said, "Bobby we're going to stay all fucking night to get this."

Ultimately, cameraman Jerry Cotts captured a passable series of Dylan-synced choruses.

But there was a remaining problem: "Ratso," Lois said, "he's got his eyes closed. Go talk to him." Dylan claimed he was trying to look at the camera. Finally, as the last words were delivered, Dylan opened his blue eyes and fixed a look. Animation replaced an eye with the moon rising in the sky which again became a blue eye in a silhouetted face and a nightingale takes flight. Perfect and dramatic. Sloman claims it was serendipity; Lois claims it was scripted.

Both Sloman and Lois agree that Columbia Records loved it. The *Los Angeles Times* called it one of the best videos ever. *Saturday Night Videos* praised it. MTV awarded it video of the year. "Ratso," Dylan said, "either I'm crazy or the world's crazy." In fact, Dylan was so dissatisfied with his closeups, he wanted Sloman to

210 / Lois maintains that Sloman had nothing to do with this phase of the production, it all being executed by his agency, Lois USA

take shots of him with an 8mm camera on the Malibu beach. "All I saw was a shot of me from my mouth to my forehead on screen. I figure, 'Isn't that somethin'? I'm paying for that?" Dylan told Paul Zollo in 1991. Lois' position was "Columbia is my client, not him," and the video stayed as shot and edited.

A longer version of the video had production credits at the end: "A Larry "Ratso" Sloman Production; produced by Chris Crowley[211] and created by George Lois; real thanks to Bill Graham and Gary Shafner."

The final word on the video comes from George Lois, "I'm not even sure I got paid for it."

Late Night With David Letterman

When Dylan agreed to the March 22 appearance on the show is not known, but he did not advise the musicians who would accompany him until a week before they would fly from LA to New York. And a different set of musicians it was. Knopfler, Clark, Sly, Robbie, and Mick Taylor were in the past, although Taylor would return for the 1984 tour. Drummer Charley Quintana had portrayed the drummer in the 'Sweetheart' video. Guitarist J. J. Holliday and bassist Tony Marisco were with Quintana in a band, The Plugz, on the Los Angeles punk music scene.[212] Quintana's girlfriend, according to Holliday, was a secretary for Gary Shafner, Dylan's assistant, and it was likely via that connection that Quintana wound up in the video. Shafner's office would call at times inviting the drummer to go Dylan's studio to jam, and he eventually brought along Holliday and Marisco.

The three did not have any idea if there was any intent by Dylan beyond informal playing and were surprised by being included in the Letterman appearance. But also surprised was the audience who witnessed the 42-year-old Dylan in a slim black suit and white tie backed by three rough-looking characters in their twenties. The gentle, reggae-tinged sound of *Infidels* was replaced by what sounded like spontaneous loud racket from an open mike night. And the band had barely rehearsed their set. From his most recent album, Dylan sang 'License to Kill' more as a threat than a sad query. 'Jokerman' blazed through

---

211 / Crowley was Lois' assistant
212 / Matthew Giles 'The Strange Story of Bob Dylan's First Letterman Appearance.' *Vulture* May 19, 2015

a striding, spirited delivery, a riveting success despite having to ignore Dylan's being handed the wrong harmonica and wandering the stage for a bit until getting the correct one.

Dylan told the band he'd call the following Monday, a call they claim did not come then or ever. While Quintana played with Dylan for a short time in the Nineties, Marisco never saw Dylan after that night.

Conclusion

CONCLUSION

This book places the spirit and perhaps the genesis of *Infidels* on the water, much like 'Jokerman', which opened the album standing on the water. The instrumentation, the placement of the vocal in the mix, the very feel of the song and its lyrics promised something different. And the promise was fulfilled.

Infidels had no lyrical or other stylistic predecessor. There were other instances of "stand alone" efforts in Dylan's recording history. *Desire* and *Street Legal* had a quality of "where did that come from?" to them. But for most albums, progression from one to another evolved in a way that one could follow. There were leaps forward, to be sure, but folk led to blues led to rock led back to folk to country-folk with a rock drum beat.

The development and production of *Infidels* came out of a perfect storm of time, place, people and mood. Dylan's sails on *Water Pearl* exposed him to language, music and ways of living. These exposures, perhaps short immersions, joined with the thoughts about the world, God and mankind that he wrote in his notebooks They were pieces of stories and found their way into songs.

Dylan's search for a celebrity producer led to Mark Knopfler, whose style also would steer the music in a certain direction. The inspired selection of Dunbar and Shakespeare for the rhythm section backbone assured a departure from straight-forward rock and roll drummers and bassists. The production staff, Neil Dorfsman and Josh Abbey, brought skill and sympathetic hands on the controls. The possibilities offered by the new digital techniques added (and some contend detracted) to the album by aiding Dylan's constant tinkering.

On that subject, the massive writing effort Dylan put in before, during and after recording is evident from the archival materials. Also evident is the spirit of a perfectionist who is frequently uncertain that what he has produced is as good as it can be. Dylan's constant wordplay was indulged and lyrics were rewritten. Mixes were adjusted. The album's title changed and the release was delayed for a new cover photograph and layout.

Often after a song is recorded and fixed, Dylan exhibits an ambivalence toward his creation. He almost seems to lose interest as his creativity drives him in new directions. This is possibly the case even as he records a song. His comments regarding 'Jokerman' having gotten away from him and others noting that 'Foot of Pride' was never finished to Dylan's liking demonstrate how difficult it is for him to maintain the same focus on a song from inspiration to completion.

In October 27, 1983, when *Infidels* was released, listeners reacted to what they heard on the recording, independent of the creativity that went into it or the uncertainty of the artist.

Reviews as noted earlier were mostly positive or enthusiastic. Sales were the best for any Dylan release since the 1979 *Slow Train Coming* and until the 1997 *Time Out of Mind*. The record was certified Gold in the U.S., and one report put sales at 750,000 units. An analytics operation with a website titled *ChartMasters* puts total physical sales as of June 2019 at two million. The album's immediate and ongoing success would doubtless have been enhanced by a stronger tour effort than the six-week European outing eight months after release, but lost opportunities cannot be reclaimed. There could have been many reasons not to tour until May 1984. Perhaps the money offered by promoters was not suitable. Perhaps Dylan did not feel he had the right group of musicians available for the road. Any number of personal reasons or obligations could enter into it.

There is a unity to *Infidels* and the unreleased material. We've previously posited that Man could be viewed as the infidel, betraying the promise of life and the earth the Lord provided. A case for the poisoned relationship between Man and Man and Man and the universe can be made in each song. Perhaps *Infidels*, with a global application, is a title better suited to the collection of songs than the more personal *Surviving in a Ruthless World* would have been. Then again, it is possible that either title were words that came at random to Dylan, with no greater meaning.

If *Infidels* had no precedent, it also had no successor. While the next album, *Empire Burlesque*, recycled some of the discards from 1983, it did not have the sound, the singing or thematic unity of *Infidels*. Dylan, who disdains copying himself, has successfully kept from duplicating what he accomplished, despite his misgivings, on *Infidels*. He certainly has gone forward with a remarkable and vibrant career. But that one moment in time was just that: a moment. With two exceptions, 2012's 'Roll On John' and 2020's 'Murder Most Foul', there is no other evidence Dylan wrote or recorded such specifically direct lyrics as 'Neighborhood Bully', 'Union Sundown', 'Clean Cut Kid' or 'Julius and Ethel' again.

All in all, *Infidels* was a port of call, not a harbor home.

CONCLUSION

Section Three:

Appendices, Information and Acknowledgements

1:

Clichés, Aphorisms and Images

A great deal of effort has been expended by many people trying to identify origins of lines in Dylan's lyrics. This list adds to that speculation, with a caveat: all of us have phrases tumbling around in our heads that we've heard in conversation, in entertainment, in worship. Without an underlined book or schedule of movies watched, it's all guesswork, at best "hmm, isn't that interesting?" "Open up yer eyes an' ears an' yer influenced." So wrote Bob Dylan in 1962 in 'My Life In A Stolen Moment'.

The following list could be expanded by reaching for tenuous, possible, could be and might be connections. What is included are the most direct.

Blind Willie McTell

"This Land is Condemned" – A Tennessee Williams one-act play was made into a movie in 1966 titled *This Property is Condemned*. New Orleans serves as the aspirational destination of the character played by Natalie Wood.

God is in His Heaven - 'Pippa Passes' a poem by Robert Browning

Don't Fall Apart on Me Tonight

"Just a minute before you leave girl/Just a minute before you touch the door.... Yesterday's just a memory." – The musical play *Damn Yankees* includes a song 'Can You Take Me High Enough' that has the words "Yesterday's just a memory/ Can we close the door."

Burning Bridges - cliché

Jokerman

"Standing on the Water" – possible allusion to miracle of walking on the water

"Casting your bread" – based on Ecclesiastes

"Fools rush in where angels fear to tread" – *An Essay on Criticism* by Alexander Pope

Clean-Cut Kid

The term "clean-cut kid" is a general colloquialism. The song itself references many clichés about Fifties/Sixties American suburban culture; i.e. baseball team, marching band, watermelon stand, Coca Cola, Wonder Bread, etc., etc., etc.

Man of Peace

"Gift of gab"

Someone's Got A Hold Of My Heart

"Eat, drink and be merry" is actually in quotation marks in the lyrics; from *Ecclesiastes 8:15*

"A lily among thorns" is from the *Song of Solomon*

"There's plenty of spies/Every street is crooked." A twenties silent film *Every Street Is Crooked* featured spies. This is probably a coincidence

"Voice crying in the wilderness" – *John 1:23* "I am the voice of one crying in the wilderness."

Sweetheart Like You

The title seems like something from a Bogart movie but, alas, does not appear to be. *What's a Nice Girl Like You Doing In a Place Like This?* is the title of a 1963 student film by Martin Scorsese. Other than Dylan once using "nice girl" in place of 'Sweetheart' in the run tape for April 18, it is a tenuous connection.

"Vanity got the best of him." Vanity is one of the so-called seven deadly sins, another of which is pride, which appears in another *Infidels* song.

"They say in your father's house, there's many mansions." Jesus says this in *John 14.2.*

"They say that patriotism is the last refuge to which a scoundrel clings." Samuel

Johnson is credited as saying this on April 7, 1775.
Steal a little and they throw you in jail/Steal a lot and they make you king."
Chung Tzu/Zhuangzi(c 360 BC): "The petty thief is imprisoned but the big thief becomes a feudal lord."

Tell Me

"Do you long to ride on that old ship of Zion?"(unpublished lyric) The 'Old Ship of Zion' is a Christian Hymn from the 1880s written by Mariah J. Cartwright.

"What means more to you/A live dog or a dead lion?"(unpublished lyric) Similar to *Ecclesiastes 9:4* "for a living dog is better than a dead lion."

Foot of Pride

Title is found in *Psalms 36:11*.

"It's like the earth just opened and swallowed him up." In *Numbers 16:21*, Korah and others fomented rebellion against Moses and "the earth opened its mouth and swallowed them."

"You know what they say about bein' nice to the right people on the way up/ Sooner or later you gonna meet them coming' down." Wilson Mizner was a twentieth century playwright, Florida developer, and con man who said, "Be nice to people on the way up because you'll meet the same people on the way down." Off topic – but not by much – he is also credited with "When you steal from one author, it's plagiarism; if you steal from many, it's research." In another probable coincidence, Mizner wrote the screenplay for the 1933 movie *Hard To Handle*.[213]

"From the stage they'll be tryin' to get water outa rocks," a miracle performed by Moses *Exodus 17: 1-7*

"They got mystery written all over their forehead," is similar to *Revelation 17:5:*

---

213 / *Hard To Handle* is the title of the HBO film memorializing Dylan's 1986 tour or Australia with Tom Petty

"On her forehead was a name written: 'Mystery, Babylon the great, the mother of harlots and abominations of the earth.'"

"Let the dead bury the dead." *Matthew 8:22*, Jesus says "let the dead bury their own dead."

I and I

"No man sees my face and lives." In *Exodus 33:20* the Lord tells Moses "You cannot see My face, for no man can see Me and live!"

"Took a stranger to teach me, to look into justice's beautiful face/And to see an eye for an eye and a tooth for a tooth." The concept of proportional justice is found in the *Code of Hammurab*i, and later in *Leviticus 24:20*. In *Matthew 5, 38, 39*, Jesus argues against such reactive justice, urging the turning of the aggrieved's cheek.

Lord Protect My Child

"There'll be a time I hear tell/When all will be well/When God and man will be reconciled." It is an adaptation of *Colossians 1:20* discussing Christ's sacrifice "And, having made peace through the blood of his cross, by him to reconcile all things unto himself; by him, I say, whether they be things in earth, or things in heaven."

General Observation

Snakes slither through the songs on *Infidels*. The album opens with a "snake in both of your fists," moves along to "King snake will crawl" and finishes with "the streets are filled with vipers." I Don't really know what to make of it, but it sticks out. Perhaps left over from "not going to get bitten by that same snake twice" from 1980[214]

In an unrelated vein(maybe not), women of lesser virtue reside in drafts of songs that in some cases are later rewritten, such as 'Jokerman's' "put him at the feet of

214 / 'Ain't Gonna Go To Hell For Anybody'

a stripper." However. "Feet of a harlot" does survive to rhyme with scarlet. 'Too Late' has bumps and grinds, along with a whore passing the hat. One version of 'Tell Me' asks if "are you someone's plaything or toy are you just like a waitress who say's 'What'll it boys?'"

2:

Images In the Jokerman Video

Standing on the water casting your bread:
Self-Portrait as The Redeemer Durer, 1500

While the eyes of the idol with the iron head:
Sumerian Idol, 2700 B.C.

Distant ships sailing into the mist:
The Slave Ship, J.M.W. Turner, 1840

You were born with a snake in both of your fists:
Minoan snake goddess, 1500 B.C.

While a hurricane was blowing:
Animation of Milton Glaser 1967 poster

Freedom just around the corner for you:
Moses, Michelangelo, 1514

But with truth so far off what good would it do?:
Man in Bondage Book of Urizen, Blake,1795

So swiftly the sun sets in the sky:
Photo of Bob Dylan at piano, 1965

You rise up and say good bye to no one:
Lamentation Over The Dead Christ, Andrea Mantegna, c. 1480

Fools rush in where angels fear to tread:
Photo of American soldiers making amphibious landing

Both of their futures so full of dread:
Photo of flag-draped casket

Shedding off one more layer of skin:

Photo sequence of Bob Dylan, 1963, 1964,
1962, 1975, 1974, 1968, 1981, 1975, 1976, 1975, 1965

You're a man of the mountains, you can Walk on the clouds:
The Delphi Charioteer, Greece 5th Century B.C.

Manipulator of crowds, you're a dream twister:
Photo of Adolph Hitler

You're going to Sodom and Gomorrah:
Film of nuclear explosion

Ain't nobody there would want to marry your sister:
Weeping Woman, Picasso, 1937

Friend to the martyr, friend to the woman of shame:
Woman and Man, Lidner, 1971

You look into the fiery furnace:
The Musicians Hell, Hieronymus Bosch, 1510

Well, the Book of Leviticus and Deuteronomy:
Jewish Illuminated Manuscript, Germany, 1300

The law of the jungle and the sea are your only teacher:
Island Man of New Guinea, Kirk, 1970

In the smoke of the twilight on a milk white steed:
The Battle of San Romano, Uccello, 1435-50

Michelangelo indeed could have carved out your features:
Statue of David, Michelangelo, 1504

Resting in the fields, far from the turbulent space:

Cow's Skull - Red, White, and Blue, Georgia O' Keefe. 1931

Half-asleep 'neath the stars with a small dog licking your face:
Chief Joseph of the New Perce, Curtis, 1903

Well, the rifleman's stalking the sick and the lame:
The Third of May 1808, Goya, 1814

Preacherman seeks the same :
The Armour of Henry VIII, 1520

Nightsticks and water cannons
tear gas padlocks, Molotov cocktails and rocks behind every curtain:
animations of jokers and demons

False hearted judges:
Muhammad Ali (as St. Sebastian), George Lois, 1968

Dying in the web that they spin:
Colossal Head, Palazzo Orsini Bomarzo, Italy

Only a matter of time til night comes stepping in :
John and Robert Kennedy, Martin Luther King at Arlington Cemetery,
montage by George Lois, 1969

(During chorus, animated The Joker from DC Comics and photo of Ronald Regan
mocking)

It's a shadowy world, skies are slippery grey :
The Scream, Munch, 1893

A woman just gave birth to a prince today:
Goddess of the Earth and Procreation, Aztec, 1400
Animations by Deros Animation

3:

Infidels Songs Performed Live

Handicapped by its tape mates having a 14-year head start when it finally sneaked into a set in 1997, 'Blind Willie McTell' made up lost ground and has been performed the most times by Dylan.

Jokerman 157 performances from May 28, 1984 – November 25, 2003
Sweetheart Like You Never performed
Neighborhood Bully Never performed
License to Kill 46 performances from May 28, 1984 – September 26, 1998
Man of Peace 41 performances from May 28, 1984 – September 19, 2000
Union Sundown 30 performances from June 20, 1986 – September 3, 1992
I and I 204 performances from May 28, 1984 – November 10, 1999
Don't Fall Apart On Me Tonight Never performed
Blind Willie McTell 226 performances from August 5, 1997 – June 17, 2017

Although 'Clean Cut Kid' was performed 68 times beginning in September 1985, it is officially an *Empire Burlesque* song and was recorded anew for that album. 'Someone's Got A Hold Of My Heart' was repurposed as 'Tight Connection To My Heart (Has Anybody Seen My Love')' for *Empire Burlesque*. It was performed 14 times from January 12, 1990 to November 17, 1993. One of the November 16 or 17, 1993 performances may someday be released when/if the *Supper Club* shows are available. None of the other songs written for and recorded at the *Infidels* sessions have been performed.

215 / Information from bobdylan.com

4:

The Sessions

Several session histories exist for *Infidels*. Danish researcher Michael Krogsgaard received approval from Dylan's New York office in the early Nineties to do a thorough research effort through all then-known materials and records, including at Sony Music and documentation at the Iron Mountain storage facility. He began publishing the results of this massive effort in the Autumn 1995 issue of the British periodical *The Telegraph*. *The Telegraph* was the Cadillac of what were and still are called "Fanzines," a limiting and almost sneering term lumping a wide variety of publications into one condescending barrel. *The Telegraph* was edited by John Bauldie, if not a man of wealth, certainly a man of wit and taste. Bauldie died on October 22, 1996 in a helicopter crash. He had been the guest of businessman Matthew Harding on a trip to see his beloved Bolton Wanderers soccer (football) team. The aircraft's pilot was not qualified for the instruments required by that evening's fog.

The articles in *The Telegraph* went as far as Part 4, covering sessions through February 15, 1980.

The spirit of *The Telegraph* was kept alive by Englishmen Mike Wyvill and John Wraith, who published the remaining five installments of Krogsgaard's research in *The Bridge*.

The world of Dylan research has an edge of competitiveness to it and author Clinton Heylin was at work on his own book. *Dylan: Behind Closed Doors - The Recording Sessions, 1960-94*, was published June 27, 1996.[216]

While Krogsgaard and Heylin did their best and significantly contributed to the knowledge of Dylan's recording history, neither had the breadth of information now available at The Bob Dylan Archive®. Further, during his research, Heylin was cut off from some of the materials Krogsgaard had available.

The information in this appendix is informed by the session sheets, tape box data, an update of information attempted around 2012 by Dylan's organization, and the generous sharing of the raw data Krogsgaard collected. It is further enhanced by the opportunity to listen (repeatedly) to the session tapes. Finally, the information provided by interviews with most of the musicians, engineers and other personnel has served to flesh out the picture.

214 / In the spirit of full disclosure, the author of this book co-authored with Paul Loeber a scathing (to put it mildly) review of Heylin's book. This appeared in the next-to-last issue of *The Telegraph* edited by Bauldie. Heylin and the author seem to have gotten beyond it

In addition to the session tapes, four compiled masters were produced. These were likely the source for the cassettes submitted to the Copyright Office. 'Jokerman', Don't Fall Apart on Me Tonight' and 'Union Sundown', have vocals and mixes from some time before the final released versions. 'I And I' has the two men waiting for "something to crack" line and also the extended playout. 'Death Is Not The End' has additional minutes of "Not the end, No, No" with Full Force after the last verse. Both the circulating and released 'Blind Willie McTell' versions are included, as are two of 'Tell Me' in two different keys – D and E. The latter has the Full Force backing vocals. 'Lord Protect My Child' is not on the compilation.

One of the key departures in the following listing is that it is based on what is heard on the tapes rather than upon what the engineers wrote at the time. This in no way is to criticize the engineers. They were operating in real time. There were very few count-ins. The 32-minute reels began and were noted at 0000 and in theory could go to 3200. The records were not kept by minutes and seconds per track. Indeed, many tracks begin out of something else going on.

For the purposes here, best efforts have been made to identify each distinct effort and assign a duration to it. Therefore, there are more 'Blind Willie McTell' and 'I and I' tracks listed than in other studies. As was said above, "best efforts."

A final departure is in identifying a number of songs that the engineer's sheets had not been able to. For example, on April 13, the recording sheets have a song titled 'Oklahoma Kansas'. In fact, this is the Woody Guthrie song 'Do Re Mi'. Where there was no reason to assign another title to what the engineers wrote down, their work was left alone and is repeated here.

The run tapes were created for historical records and are covered within the book narrative.

They are not included in the Session listings.

April 11, 1983
Rundown Instrumental, 1:38,
Rundown 2, 0:03,
Rundown 3, 0:34,
Rundown 4, 0:21,
Rundown 5, 0:36,

Rundown 6, 0:33,

Rundown 7, 1:00,

Rundown Piano, 7:45,

Rundown 8 – vocal tryout, 4:28,

Rundown Piano, Vocal at 6:57, 9:44,

Blind Willie McTell, 0:59, Reel 2

Blind Willie McTell, 0:31, Reel 2

Blind Willie McTell, 0:19, Reel 2

Blind Willie McTell, 5:32, Reel 2

Blind Willie McTell, 1:08, Reel 2

Blind Willie McTell, 0:27, Reel 2

Blind Willie McTell, 5:01, Reel 2

Blind Willie McTell, 0:32, Reel 2

Oh, Babe, 7:39, Reel 2

Blind Willie McTell, 1:56, Reel 2

Blind Willie McTell, 6:43, Reel 2 Circulating as "full band" version

Instrumental Jam, 3:10, Reel 3

Don't Fall Apart on Me Tonight, 0:41, Reel 3

Don't Fall Apart on Me Tonight, 0:19, Reel 3

Don't Fall Apart on Me Tonight, 11:52, Reel 3

Don't Fall Apart on Me Tonight, 2:28, Reel 3

Don't Fall Apart on Me Tonight, 1:06, Reel 3

Don't Fall Apart on Me Tonight, 6:40, Reel 3

Don't Fall Apart on Me Tonight, 2:57, Reel 3

April 12, 1983

Don't Fall Apart on Me Tonight, 6:08, Reel 4

Don't Fall Apart on Me Tonight, 6:34, Reel 4

Don't Fall Apart on Me Tonight, 0:42, Reel 4

Don't Fall Apart on Me Tonight, 5:34, Reel 4

Don't Fall Apart on Me Tonight, 0:14, Reel 4

Don't Fall Apart on Me Tonight, 4:15, Reel 4

Don't Fall Apart on Me Tonight, 0:49, Reel 4

Don't Fall Apart on Me Tonight, 5:52, Reel 4

Don't Fall Apart on Me Tonight, 6:06, Reel 5
Don't Fall Apart on Me Tonight, 0:14, Reel 5
Don't Fall Apart on Me Tonight, 0:24, Reel 5
Don't Fall Apart on Me Tonight, 0:20, Reel 5
Don't Fall Apart on Me Tonight, 0:17, Reel 5
Don't Fall Apart on Me Tonight, 6:26, Reel 5 Released on *Infidels* after overdubs
Don't Fall Apart on Me Tonight, 0:14, Reel 5

April 13, 1983
Jokerman, 5:16, Reel 6
Slow Try Baby, 6:02, Reel 6
Blues, 2:05, Reel 6
Columbus Georgia, 2:15, Reel 6
Couple More Years, 1:37, Reel 6
Do Re Mi, 3:28, Reel 6
Tuning (Jokerman), 0:22, Reel 6
Jokerman, 0:41, Reel 6
Jokerman, 2:37, Reel 6
Blues, 7:43, Reel 6
Jokerman, 6:44, Reel 7
Noodling/Jokerman, 0:43, Reel 7
Jokerman, 7:42, Reel 7 With the next take, edited and overdubbed, released on *Infidels*
Jokerman, 6:02, Reel 7 With preceding take, edited and overdubbed, released on *Infidels*
noodling, 0:05, Reel 7
License to Kill, 3:45, Reel 7 Released on *Infidels*

April 14, 1983
Clean-Cut Kid, 7:18, Reel 8 Circulating
Clean-Cut Kid (punch in), 1:18, Reel 8
noodling, 0:26, Reel 8
Clean-Cut Kid, 7:06, Reel 8
This Was My Love, 6:11, Reel 8

Man of Peace, 2:03, Reel 8

Man of Peace, 0:22, Reel 8

noodling, 0:19, Reel 8

Man of Peace, 6:44, Reel 8 Released with overdubs on *Infidels*

Jokerman Alt. Rough Mix, 7:10, Reel 9

Jokerman - later Rough Mix, 7:18, Reel 9

April 15

He'll Have to Go, 1:15, Reel 10

Don't Fly Unless It's Safe, 5:38, Reel 10 Circulating

Clean-Cut Kid, 9:02, Reel 10

Jesus Met The Woman at the Well, 4:11, Reel 10

Half-Finished Song, 0:55, Reel 10

Half-Finished Song, 3:19, Reel 10

16 Tons, 6:49, Reel 10

Clean-Cut Kid, 6:25, Reel 11

Clean-Cut Kid, 1:05, Reel 11

Clean-Cut Kid, 2:08, Reel 11

It's Too Late, 4:01, Reel 11

Clean-Cut Kid, 7:30, Reel 11

The Circle Game, 0:36, Reel 11

Sittin' Here in Limbo, 1:50, Reel 11

April 16, 1983

Bluesy Jam: Slow, 4:26, Reel 12

Bluesy Jam: Bluesier, 18:17, Reel 12

Bluesy Jam: Pickup Again, 9:12, Reel 12

Dadada Grateful Dead, 5:22, Reel 13

Reggae Toms Toms Jam, 8:20, Reel 13

Bob Said Tape This, 7:08, Reel 13

Mark Soop Pick Up, 4:32, Reel 13

Oh, Susannah!(?), 2:13, Reel 13

Jamming, 3:02, Reel 13

Jamming, 1:22, Reel 13

Jamming, 0:50, Reel 14

Jamming, 0:40, Reel 14

Dark Groove, 9:19, Reel 14

Jamming, organ joins, 0:55, Reel 14

Someone's Got A Hold of My Heart, 0:32, Reel 14

Norwegian Wood, 0:37, Reel 14

Someone's Got A Hold of My Heart, 0:08, Reel 14

Someone's Got A Hold of My Heart, 1:50, Reel 14

Bob Picking, 0:37, Reel 14

Someone's Got A Hold of My Heart, 3:45, Reel 14

Someone's Got A Hold of My Heart, 6:34, Reel 14

Someone's Got A Hold of My Heart, 2:52, Reel 14

Someone's Got AHold of My Heart, 6:11, Reel 15

Noodling, 0:36, Reel 15

Blues (Boogie?), 3:15, Reel 15

Unnamed Instrumental, 5:04, Reel 15

Piano and guitar notes, 0:07, Reel 15

Dark Groove Warmup, 0:35, Reel 15

Noodling, 1:28, Reel 15

Dark Groove, 5:27, Reel 15 Circulating in highly edited form

Instrumental, 2:48, Reel 15

April 18, 1983

Sweetheart Like You, 3:35, Reel 16

Sweetheart Like You, 2:11, Reel 16

Sweetheart Like You, 0:12, Reel 16

Sweetheart Like You, 0:18, Reel 16

Sweetheart Like You , 0:26, Reel 16

Sweetheart Like You, 1:02, Reel 16

Sweetheart Like You, 4:34, Reel 16

Sweetheart Like You, 0:11, Reel 16

Sweetheart Like You, 0:22, Reel 16

Sweetheart Like You, 0:13, Reel 16

Sweetheart Like You, 3:52, Reel 16

Sweetheart Like You, 0:11, Reel 16

Sweetheart Like You, 0:36, Reel 16

Laugh, 0:03, Reel 16

Sweetheart Like You, 0:15, Reel 16

Sweetheart Like You, 4:39, Reel 16 With many edits and overdubs, released On *Infidels*

Sweetheart Like You, 0:02, Reel 16

Sweetheart Like You, 0:08, Reel 16

Sweetheart Like You, 5:23, Reel 16

blank, 0:03, Reel 16

Sweetheart Like You, 1:11, Reel 17

Sweetheart Like You, 0:08, Reel 17

Sweetheart Like You, 0:25, Reel 17

Sweetheart Like You, 4:02, Reel 17

Sweetheart Like You, 0:06, Reel 17

Sweetheart Like You, 0:30, Reel 17

Sweetheart Like You, 0:11, Reel 17

Sweetheart Like You , 5:18, Reel 18

Blind Willie McTell, 0:30, Reel 18

Blind Willie McTell, 0:48, Reel 18

Blind Willie McTell, 5:20, Reel 18

Blind Willie McTell, 7:38, Reel 18

Blind Willie McTell, 0:01, Reel 18

Blind Willie McTell, 0:36, Reel 18

April 19, 1983

Neighborhood Bully, 1:15, Reel 19

Just Run Tape For a Minute on This Thing, 0:26, Reel 19

Neighborhood Bully, 1:31, Reel 19

Neighborhood Bully, 0:22, Reel 19

Neighborhood Bully, 0:41, Reel 19

Neighborhood Bully, 1:21, Reel 19

Neighborhood Bully, 0:57, Reel 19

Neighborhood Bully, 1:11, Reel 19

Neighborhood Bully, 0:53, Reel 19

Neighborhood Bully, 0:55, Reel 19
Neighborhood Bully, 5:15, Reel 19
Neighborhood Bully(with horns), 5:03, Reel 19 Horns edited out for release
Neighborhood Bully (handclaps), 5:02, Reel 19
Neighborhood Bully, 0:04, Reel 19
Green Onions, 5:49, Reel 20
dead space, 0:31, Reel 20
Love You Too (Jam), 6:15, Reel 20
Trees Hannibal Alps, 15:41, Reel 20
Guitar Picking, 2:43, Reel 20

April 20, 1983
This Was My Love (12 String End), 6:35, Reel 21
bad split, 0:03, Reel 21
Robbie Sly Aquarium, 17:16, Reel 21
BG Boogie, 4:40, Reel 21
This Was My Love (falsetto), 1:26, Reel 21
This Was My Love, 4:20, Reel 22
This Was My Love, 3:44, Reel 22
This Was My Love, 1:36, Reel 22
This Was My Love, 0:11, Reel 22
This Was My Love, 2:20, Reel 22
This Was My Love, 0:09, Reel 22
This Was My Love, 4:05, Reel 22
This Was My Love, 0:27, Reel 22
This Was My Love, 4:19, Reel 22
This Was My Love, 4:27, Reel 22 Circulating
This Was My Love, 0:56, Reel 22
Across the Borderline, 2:15, Reel 23
Across the Borderline, 3:22, Reel 23
Across the Borderline, 4:25, Reel 23

April 21, 1983
Tell Me, 2:29, Reel 24

Tell Me, 1:11, Reel 24

Tell Me, 4:44, Reel 24

Tell Me, 0:40, Reel 24

Tell Me, 5:15, Reel 24

Tell Me, 0:18, Reel 24

Tell Me, 0:24, Reel 24

Tell Me, 5:03, Reel 24

Tell Me, 0:48, Reel 24

Tell Me, 0:09, Reel 24

Tell Me, 0:13, Reel 24

Tell Me, 4:55, Reel 24 Edited, overdubbed, *Bootleg Series 1-3*

Tell Me , 5:16, Reel 25

Tell Me, 6:58, Reel 25 Circulating

April 22, 1983

Warm Up, 4:18, Reel 26

Too Late, 1:58, Reel 26

Instrumental, 5:02, Reel 26

Too Late, 1:55, Reel 26

Too Late, 6:39, Reel 26

Too Late, 0:39, Reel 26

Too Late , 4:07, Reel 26

Too Late, 3:09, Reel 26

Too Late, 1:12, Reel 27

Too Late, 6:10, Reel 27

Too Late (Rock Jam), 2:06,

Reel 27 noodling, 0:48, Reel 27

Too Late (Reggae Jam), 5:00,

Reel 27 noodling with tex-mex feel, 0:34,

Reel 27 Twelve Days of Christmas, 2:12,

Reel 27 Choo Choo Boogie, 4:59, Reel 27

Jam with Synth, 0:38, Reel 27

Silent Night, 3:55, Reel 27

Glory to the King (Adeste Fideles), 0:35, Reel 28

Lovers Concerto, 2:02, Reel 28
Dark As A Dungeon, 2:52, Reel 28

April 23, 1983

Too Late, 0:30, Reel 29
Too Late, 6:27, Reel 29
Too Late, 8:15, Reel 29
Too Late, 0:14, Reel 29
Too Late, 1:16, Reel 29
Too Late , 0:29, Reel 29
Too Late, 0:22, Reel 29
Too Late, 3:02, Reel 29
null, 0:01, Reel 29
Too Late, 0:19, Reel 29
Too Late, 8:56, Reel 29
Too Late, 1:05, Reel 30
Piano warmup, 1:17, Reel 30
Too Late, 1:00, Reel 30
Jam with Piano, 3:25, Reel 30
Too Late, 1:09, Reel 30
Too Late, 8:09, Reel 30
Too Late, 0:13, Reel 30
Too Late (Reggae), 6:25, Reel 30

April 25, 1983

Foot of Pride, 6:40, Reel 31
Foot of Pride, 0:32, Reel 31
Foot of Pride, 0:33, Reel 31
Foot of Pride, 6:45, Reel 31
Foot of Pride, 0:16, Reel 31
Foot of Pride, 0:13, Reel 31
Foot of Pride , 2:29, Reel 31
Foot of Pride, 7:47, Reel 31
Foot of Pride, 7:37, Reel 32

Foot of Pride, 1:55, Reel 32
Foot of Pride, 0:28, Reel 32
Someone's Got A Hold Of My Heart, 2:47, Reel 32
Someone's Got A Hold Of My Heart, 0:17, Reel 32
Some's Got A Hold Of My Heart, 0:35, Reel 32
Someone's Got A Hold Of My Heart, 0:27, Reel 32
Someone's Got A Hold Of My Heart, 5:54, Reel 32 With overdubs, *The Bootleg Series 1-3*
Foot of Pride, 1:15, Reel 32
Foot of Pride, 2:00, Reel 33
Foot of Pride, 0:43, Reel 33
Foot of Pride, 0:52, Reel 33
Foot of Pride, 6:41, Reel 33
Foot of Pride, 0:21, Reel 33
Foot of Pride, 7:58, Reel 33

April 26, 1983
Foot of Pride, 0:56, Reel 34
Foot of Pride, 0:13, Reel 34
Foot of Pride, 0:57, Reel 34
Foot of Pride, 5:54, Reel 34
Foot of Pride, 0:09, Reel 34
Foot of Pride, 5:09, Reel 34
Foot of Pride, 7:47, Reel 34
Vocal Overdubs, 3:15, Reel 34
Wildwood Flower, 0:47, Reel 34
Mark Picking, 0:16, Reel 34
Wildwood Flower, 0:58, Reel 34
Forever My Darling, 1:30, Reel 34
Someone's Got A Hold Of My Heart, 0:54, Reel 35
Someone's Got A Hold Of My Heart, 0:46, Reel 35
Someone's Got A Hold Of My Heart, 5:22, Reel 35
Someone's Got A Hold Of My Heart, 5:23, Reel 35 *Bootleg Series 1-3*
Choo Choo Boogie (Part II), 2:32, Reel 35
Cold, Cold Heart, 1:49, Reel 35

Cold, Cold Heart, 4:29, Reel 35
I'm Movin' On, 1:06, Reel 35
I'm Movin' On, 3:30, Reel 35
KIM, 3:42, Reel 36

April 27, 1983
From Paul, 3:14, Reel 36
Foot of Pride, 1:15, Reel 37
Foot of Pride, 0:28, Reel 37
Foot of Pride, 0:21, Reel 37
Foot of Pride, 7:20, Reel 37
Foot of Pride, 7:40, Reel 37
Union Sundown, 1:20, Reel 37
Union Sundown , 3:11, Reel 37
Union Sundown, 5:17, Reel 37 Circulating
I And I, 1:29, Reel 38
I And I, 1:01, Reel 38
I And I, 5:42, Reel 38
I And I, 0:27, Reel 38
I And I, 2:08, Reel 38
I And I, 2:58, Reel 38
I And I, 1:14, Reel 38
I And I, 0:39, Reel 38
I And I, 0:26, Reel 38
I And I, 0:20, Reel 38
I And I, 0:14, Reel 38
I And I, 7:22, Reel 38 Overdubs, edits, released on *Infidels*
I And I/Julius and Ethel, 2:25, Reel 39
I And I, 0:20, Reel 39
I And I, 5:35, Reel 39
Julius and Ethel, 0:05, Reel 39
Julius and Ethel, 3:14, Reel 39
Julius and Ethel, 5:54, Reel 39 Circulating in edited form

April 29, 1983

Harmonica Jam, 4:20, Reel 40

Harmonica Jam, 8:21, Reel 40

Don't Drive No Chevy, 3:15, Reel 40

Harmonica Jam, 10:01, Reel 40

Don't Drink No Chevy, 0:47, Reel 40

Don't Drive No Chevy, 2:51, Reel 40

How Many Days, 1:58, Reel 40

How Many Days, 6:32, Reel 41

Guitar Strums, 1:10, Reel 41

Two Guitar noodling, 1:04, Reel 41

Jam, 6:31, Reel 41

Up Tempo Jam, 3:35, Reel 41

Guitar, Harp Jam, 3:04, Reel 42

Warmup, 1:02, Reel 42

Unknown, 2:18, Reel 42

Unknown, 6:08, Reel 42

Jazz Runs, 0:47, Reel 42

Home on the Range, 3:04, Reel 42

Buttons and Bows, 1:05, Reel 42

Buttons And Bows, 0:59, Reel 42

Buttons and Bows, 0:13, Reel 42

Gonna Wash That Man Right Out of My Hair, 0:35, Reel 42

Buttons and Bows, 4:47, Reel 42

End of Buttons, 0:04, Reel 42

Foot of Pride Instrumental, 2:28, Reel 42

Foot of Pride, 0:33, Reel 43

Foot of Pride, 6:24, Reel 43

Foot of Pride, 0:26, Reel 43

Foot of Pride, 0:56, Reel 43

Foot of Pride, 1:13, Reel 43

Foot of Pride, 0:49, Reel 43

Foot of Pride, 1:11, Reel 43

Foot of Pride, 1:38, Reel 43
Foot of Pride, 3:39, Reel 43
Foot of Pride, 0:15, Reel 43
Foot of Pride, 6:22, Reel 43 *Bootleg Series 1-3*

May 2, 1983
Lord Protect My Child, 5:54, Reel 44
Angel Flying Too Close To The Ground, 1:15, Reel 44
Angel Flying Too Close To The Ground, 3:52, Reel 44
Angel Flying Too Close To The Ground, 4:26, Reel 44
Angel Flying Too Close To The Ground, 3:51, Reel 44
noodling, 0:28, Reel 44
Angel Flying Too Close To The Ground, 0:24, Reel 44
Angel Flying Too Close To The Ground, 4:46, Reel 44
Angel Flying Too Close To The Ground, 5:36, Reel 44
Lord Protect My Child, 3:36, Reel 45
Lord Protect My Child, 0:18, Reel 45
Lord Protect My Child, 0:26, Reel 45
Lord Protect My Child, 4:10, Reel 45
Lord Protect My Child, 0:48, Reel 45
Lord Protect My Child, 0:32, Reel 45
Lord Protect My Child, 4:05, Reel 45
Lord Protect My Child, 1:23, Reel 45
Lord Protect My Child, 4:56, Reel 45 Released on *The Bootleg Series 1-3*, edited
Lord Protect My Child, 0:47, Reel 45
Lord Protect My Child, 5:39, Reel 45
Lord Protect My Child, 0:18, Reel 46
Lord Protect My Child, 5:02, Reel 46
Union Sundown, 0:18, Reel 46
Union Sundown, 6:27, Reel 46
Union Sundown, 7:21, Reel 46 Circulating
Green Green Grass of Home, 2:15, Reel 46
Green Green Grass of Home, 3:54, Reel 46
Jam Groove, 1:18, Reel 46

Baby, What You Want Me To Do, 8:13, Reel 47
Union Sundown, 0:17, Reel 47
Union Sundown, 0:13, Reel 47
Union Sundown, 0:11, Reel 47
Union Sundown, 6:55, Reel 47 Released on *Infidels*, edited and overdubbed
Lord Protect My Child, 1:13, Reel 47
Lord Protect My Child, 5:26, Reel 47
Death Is Not The End, 0:48, Reel 47
Death Is Not The End, 0:49, Reel 47
Death Is Not The End, 0:48, Reel 47
Death Is Not The End, 7:23, Reel 47 Released on *Down In The Groove*
Angel Flying Too Close To The Ground, 2:11, Reel 48
Angel Flying Too Close To The Ground, 1:11, Reel 48
Angel Flying Too Close To The Ground, 3:33, Reel 48
Angel Flying Too Close To The Ground, 0:33, Reel 48
Angel Flying To Close To The Ground, 0:11, Reel 48
Angel Flying Too Close To The Ground, 0:17, Reel 48
Angel Flying Too Close To The Ground, 1:02, Reel 48
Angel Flying Too Close To The Ground, 5:36, Reel 48 Single release, non-US

May 5, 1983
Blind Willie McTell, 1:05, Reel 49
Blind Willie McTell, 0:12, Reel 49
Blind Willie McTell, 6:09, Reel 49 Released on *The Bootleg Series 1-3*
Blind Willie McTell, 5:57, Reel 49

Publisher And Copyright Information

Blind Willie Mctell
Copyright © 1983 by Special Rider Music

Don't Fall Apart On Me Tonight
Copyright © 1983 by Special Rider Music.

Jokerman
Copyright © 1983 by Special Rider Music

License To Kill
Copyright © 1983 by Special Rider Music

Clean-Cut Kid
Copyright © 1984 by Special Rider Music

Man Of Peace
Copyright © 1983 by Special Rider Music

Someone's Got A Hold Of My Heart
Copyright ©1983 by Special Rider Music

Sweetheart Like You
Copyright © 1983 by Special Rider Music

Neighborhood Bully
Copyright © 1983 by Special Rider Music

Tell Me
Copyright © 1983 by Special Rider Music

Foot Of Pride
Copyright © 1983 by Special Rider Music

Union Sundown
Copyright © 1983 by Special Rider Music

I And I
Copyright © 1983 by Special Rider Music

Julius And Ethel (unpublished)
Copyright © 1983 Special Rider Music

Lord Protect My Child
Copyright © 1983 by Special Rider Music

Death Is Not The End
Copyright © 1988 by Special Rider Music

Too Late (unpublished) *
Copyright © 1983 by Special Rider Music.
Additional lyrics © 2020 by Special Rider Music

Notebooks (unpublished) *
Copyright © 2020 by Bob Dylan

Jokerman Alternate Lyrics (unpublished) *
Copyright © 1983 by Special Rider Music.
Additional lyrics © 2020 by Special Rider Music

I And I Alternate Lyrics (unpublished) *
Copyright © 1983 by Special Rider Music.
Additional lyrics © 2020 by Special Rider Music

Sweetheart Like You Alternate Lyrics (unpublished) *
Copyright © 1983 by Special Rider Music.
Additional lyrics © 2020 by Special Rider Music

Tell Me Alternate Lyrics (unpublished) *
Copyright © 1983 by Special Rider Music.
Additional lyrics © 2020 by Special Rider Music

Someone's Got A Hold Of My Heart Alernate Lyrics (unpublished) *
Copyright © 1983 by Special Rider Music.
Additional lyrics © 2020 by Special Rider Music

Neighborhood Bully Alternate Lyrics (unpublished) *
Copyright © 1983 by Special Rider Music.

Acknowlegements

This section is personal, and as such you will find the word "I" throughout. I have to use "I" to get to the proper gratitude.

This book is the result and product of over 50 years of interest in the music, lyrics, and persona of Bob Dylan. I did not know it at the start, but all along I was following a path that demanded I explore deeply an album that intrigued me from the first note and share what I learned and thought. Though inevitability is perceived in hindsight, the combination of having just concluded one job and the coincident establishment of The Bob Dylan Archive® in Tulsa, Oklahoma could be seen as destiny, something unavoidable for me.

The journey began in earnest, after three years of casual album listening, when I was working on the student newspaper at Miami University in Oxford, Ohio. Publishers sent in books they hoped would be reviewed in school papers and one of these, in early 1966, was a book called *Folk-Rock: The Bob Dylan Story*. It was a Dell paperback book authored by Sy and Barbara Ribakove. No one at the paper seemed interested, so I took it and read it. I did not review it, but I found it fascinating. That July, the *Saturday Evening Post* had a cover story on Dylan, one which he celebrated by crashing his motorcycle within days of publication and disappearing into several years of mystery.

I made liberal use of the Reader's Guide and cranked out one term paper, one master's Thesis, and one book based on Dylan's work through early 1965. I was encouraged by my advisor, Dr. Ralph Stone on both the paper and thesis. On the thesis front, both of us had to overcome the opposition of the History Department Chair, Dr. Harris Warren, who felt Dylan an unworthy subject. In 2016 it was delightful to revel in the reflected validation when Dylan was awarded the Nobel Prize.

During the first decade of my immersion, those who helped in various ways included Tom Friedman, Harvey Pillersdorf, Alan Weberman, Shelly Livson, Randy Mixter, Rick Fry and John Paige. An article in *The Washington Post* opened my eyes to bootleg recordings. It turned out Weberman would make copies of material for the cost of the cassettes and a willingness to listen to his mad theories. In 1978, I discovered a broader group of tape collectors and that led to a copy of the *Infidels* tape mentioned in the beginning of this book. Those that fed the tape hunger included Jerry Weddle, Bob Heyer, Nat Ayer, Christian Behrens, Glen Dundas and Mitch Barth. One day when I was in New York on actual, real business, I bussed over to Little Ferry, New Jersey and met future Minnesota land baron Bill Pagel. This was around 1983, and his collection at that time was staggering

In the mid-Eighties, I began writing occasional articles that appeared in *The Telegraph* and *Look Back*. The latter allowed me to exercise attempts at humorous writing. *The Telegraph* had its lighthearted moments but was a journal of serious discussion on Dylan.

Writing the articles put me in communication with the delightfully provocative John Bauldie. as well as Ian Woodward, Dave Dingle, and the energy source named Clinton Heylin. Contemporaneously, *Isis* magazine became a must-read for facts and opinion, ably shepherded by Derek Barker and Tracy Barker. Derek connected me with Mark Neeter at Red Planet and, voila, this book.

My views were sharpened and broadened by conversation—which continues to this day—with friend and sometime collaborator Paul Loeber. Paul is a generation younger and followed tours and gathered tapes and information so intently for a dozen years that his interest in more current Dylan is diminished. He remains a good and true sounding board, and though his political views vex me, the value of our discussions is immeasurable.

Mitch Blank was and is a more occasional contact, but a constant as I seek facts. To paraphrase Dylan's 1968 *Sing Out* interview, he does not reveal all he knows or share all he sees. He has been a help for years and always a friend. And while we are in New York, Larry "Ratso" Sloman deserves a mention. You'll find him quoted in this book and his *On the Road with Bob Dylan* is essential. I get to see Dan Levy infrequently, although he did introduce me years ago to "cousin" Geoff Gans. Sean Wilentz shared meals, concerts, and viewpoints.

As noted earlier, time and the availability of archival materials allowed this book to be pursued. Perhaps the final push came when Dr. Richard Thomas gave a talk in Sarasota, FL which previewed his *Why Bob Dylan Matters* book. He came at the story he wanted to tell in a way that lit the spark. So, I contacted the The Bob Dylan Archive® to propose an area of study.

The requests went to "Librarian." This is a minimal description of Dr. Mark Davidson, the archivist, guide, juggler, preserver, organizer, and protector of the most valuable collection in contemporary music. A researcher could never be more blessed than to work with someone like Mark. He is constantly in motion and none of it is wasted. He has many things going on at once and handles them without complaint. Well, most of the time.

When mildewed sacks of fan mail from 1966 are there to be sorted the same day five researchers arrive, and Wilco wants to be shown around—it gets challenging. But, bottom line, I could not have written this book without Mark. He has gone way above and way beyond in helping.

At Tulsa, I met another superball of activity, Michael Chaiken, the Curator of the archive. He told me my book had to be written, and since he obviously knows his subject, I did as he said. There is never enough time to spend with Michael, so get it while you can.

In my trips to Tulsa, it was a pleasure to meet and speak with Sean Latham, Ken Levit, Steve Higgins, Linda Higgins, and visitors Amanda Petrusich, Anne Margaret Daniel, and Robert Polito. They helped me continue the spirit of being a historian and writer. Renee Harvey, Librarian in a different subject area at Tulsa's Gilcrease Museum, always provided a warm welcome and sustenance.

I was pleased with both the number of people who agreed to be interviewed and the generous time they gave in answering my questions. My deep thanks go to Alan Clark, Neil Dorfsman, Sly Dunbar, Robbie Shakespeare, Josh Abbey, Ed Bicknell, Chris Bowman, Larry Sloman, Arma Andon and George Lois. Josh Abbey deserves additional appreciation. He was a friendly source of information beyond an initial interview and answered questions up through the writing of the final draft and proofing of the book

There are some friends not mentioned here. They know "how come" and of my affection and appreciation for them all.

Thanks to Mark Neeter for bringing this to completion in book form. I could not have undertaken or completed this book without love and support at home. My sons, Jeremy and Danny, lived through the experience of many children – car rides with the latest album or tape playing instead of what they would have chosen on the radio. "Not Bob," was a common plea. I do not think Jeremy would object if I noted that Danny was a bit more on the same passion level as I regarding Dylan. At the same time they and their wives, Lisa and Colleen, have encouraged me in my writing. Their Aunt Ginny did the cover design for my first book and has followed my efforts from Italy. Colleen Gans advised me on the publishing agreement.

Diane Gans has given me the best support possible in my nearly two years of work, on our dime, in producing the book. She edited and proofed the draft as she did on the thesis – and her very professional skills have made it far better than it was. Wives often do not tell husbands that they are proud of them. But what they tell others comes bouncing back, and I, for one, love those moments. And, I love you, Diane.

Index